HOW MANY
BELIEVERS
WILL MAKE HEAVEN?

BY
DOROTHY PRINCEWILL

AuthorHouse™
1663 Liberty Drive
Bloomington, IN 47403
www.authorhouse.com
Phone: 833-262-8899

Unless otherwise indicated, Bible quotations are from the HOLY SCRIPTURE.
Scripture marked KJV and NKJV are taken from King James and New King James Version. Copyright in 1982 by Thomas Nelson, Inc. Used
with permission. All rights reserved. Scriptures marked NLT are taken from New Living Translation. Copyright in 1996 by Tyndale House
Publishers, Inc. Wheaton, Illinois. Used with permission. Scriptures marked ESV are taken from English Standard Version. All rights reserved.

ISBN: 979-8-8230-3300-8 (sc)
ISBN: 979-8-8230-3301-5 (e)

Print information available on the last page.

Published by AuthorHouse 02/10/2025

authorHOUSE®

CONTENTS

DEDICATION

TO GOD ALMIGHTY, TO THE LORD JESUS CHRIST, THE SON OF THE HIGHEST GOD, OUR EMMANUEL, OUR REDEEMER, OUR COMFORTER, COUNCELOR, THE LION OF TRIBE OF JUDA, THE LORD OF SABOAT, THE PRINCE OF PEACE, AND THE SOON COMING KING.

ACKNOWLEDGMENTS

TO ALMIGHTY GOD----

First, I want to give GOD all the glory and honor for HIS love, faithfulness, kindness, loving care, provision, and protection. From the day I was born, HIS able HANDS have been in my life. In all my life HE has been gracious, merciful, and faithful to me.

To my Husband, Dr. Joseph----

To: The husband of my youth. We have been married for over 43 years. We have gone through many waters and by the special grace of GOD; we have weathered many storms together. There have been many days of going through the adversity of life; nevertheless, the LORD saw us through and continued to see us through all the adversity of life. There are many days of impressive triumph and fulfillment; there have been numerous periods of overwhelming warfare and dissuasion. Daddy, I cannot thank GOD enough for you. You are more than a blessing to me. You are an answer to my prayer.

To: All my GOD given three sons and my three daughters in LOVE: I could not ask anything more from GOD. I thank GOD for all your love and support. GOD has been faithful to me.

To: All, my grandchildren. You are my GOD given joy.

To: My Church Family; Assembles of GOD Church. No 1 Afipko Street, Port Harcourt, Rivers State, Nigeria; To Late Rev. Joe Peterside.

To: Assembles of GOD Church. No 5 Emole Street, Mile 2 Diobu, Port Harcourt, Rivers State; Late Rev. Princewill Owoh and Rev. Osumaya.

To: All Scripture Union members; Moscow Road, Port Harcourt, Rivers State, Nigeria. The history of my Christian life will not be complete without you as a group. Thanks to all of you.

To Dr. Joseph Goin. My God-given brother. You are my encourager, advisor, and my mentor. Word of mouth cannot express or quantify the love you have shown to me and the entire family. Only GOD will reward you and entire family IJMN AMEN. You have impacted my life in so many ways, and I want you to know that you are forever appreciated.

To: African Christian Fellowship U.S.A.

My Christian firm foundation started from what I learnt under their teaching, all the above-mentioned BODY of CHRIST. I am eternally grateful for teaching me unadulterated WORD of

GOD. I strongly believe that it has sustained me in all these years of walking with the LORD. Thank you for your love, care, and support in my life.

To: My two GOD given daughters------ Mrs. Sarah Igboji and Mrs. Dupe Edeoga (B.J.)

To: All my GOD Children.

To: Late Pastor Sam & his wife Benita Umunna. Wonderful couple. The first meal we had in Chicago was in your house the very first day we arrived in Chicago on April 21st, 1990. You assisted us in securing accommodation. You showed me around the grocery stores and train station. You did so much for us to settle in Chicago. Thank you and your lovely wife for all your help and love you showed to us. May soul rest in peace. We appreciate you and your entire family. May the LORD bless all of you.

To: Sister Merechi Selina Ogbonnia. Where will I start to say something about you, my beloved sister? You are the first ACF member to invite our family to your house upon arrival in Chicago in 1990, from Atlanta, Georgia. You are always there for me and the family. With all my health challenges, you will come to see me in the snow or sunshine. With my multiple hospital admissions, you are there all the time. My sister, I cannot innumerate your love and care for me. All I have to say is thank you and may the LORD continue to grant you good health and long life IJMN Amen.

To: Minister Kunle & Dr. Mrs. Bola Coker. My brother and my sister, I do not know where to start to express my gratitude to both of you. You have shown me so much love that words of mouth cannot express it. Just to let you know that my prayer for both of you is to be mightily blessed by our FATHER IN HEAVEN. The entire family appreciate you and yours.

To: Mrs. Gillian Okoye. Sister Gillian, thank you so much. You know when I am hungry, and you know when I am down. Your love for me and the entire family is so great. You are not a friend, but you are my younger sister. We both cling to each other the very first time we met over 26 years ago. You still love me despite all my flaws. Thanks a lot.

To: Mr. Joseph & Mrs. Eme Ikafia ---Your love and care for me and my family are highly appreciated. May bless you and the entire family.

To Dr. Sunday & Mrs. Vicky Olayinka ---GOD brought these two families together for a special purpose. You two have been a blessing to me and the entire family in many ways. In those difficult and health challenging times, you call and pray with us is cherished more than anything. Thank you very much.

To: Rev. Dr. Sunday & Mrs. Grace Banwhot. Thank you, Daddy, and Darling for your unconditional love for me and the entire family.

To: Dr. Mrs. Deborah Omelogu-------Mommy "D" as our family calls you, my prayer partner you have been a blessing to me and the entire family. You are always there for my children and grandchildren. The Princewill family calls you mummy "D" because of the roles you have played in our family and still doing at what you are best.

To Dr. Josephine --After this revelation, I shared this thought with my sister and prayer partner. She told me that this is a scary question. Both of us spent a lot of time trying to analyze the implication of this question. We were both scared. I told her that GOD'S willing; I will author a book on this question. I thank GOD for your encouragement and input my sister. Thank you, Dr. Josephine. Thank you, my prayer partner, my sister, and my cheer leader for everything I do. I can always call you any time for prayer and you are always there for me and the entire family. I love you so much.

To: All Women of Divine Purpose

You have put up with me for so many years, believing in the call of GOD upon my life and allowing me to accomplish it through your love, prayers, and support. Thank you for your sisterhood and friendship. I love you and cherish your sisterhood and your prayers.

To: All Wailing Women Worldwide and U.S.A. 7 A.M. Watch Family. Wailing Women Chicago. Thank you all so much. Each one of you has been a blessing to me. You have impacted my life in so many ways. Thank you for believing in me and the responsibility you trusted in me. I want all of you to know that I dearly love each one of you. Thank you all so much.

To: my Pastor Scott Tomatz; Radius Church (Assembly of GOD Church). Pastor Scott, thank you for preaching the WORD OF GOD with boldness and without any fear.

INTRODUCTION

One morning in October of 2022, I woke up with the question how many believers will make Heaven? For this question, I am not able to answer because it is beyond my ability. Only GOD HIMSELF can answer this subjective question! "The question came directly to me. "How many believers will actually make it to HEAVEN?" This question is really complicated for me to answer. I am the least person for this kind of question to come to. I have no idea who will make HEAVEN or who will not make HEAVEN! Is only GOD ALMIGHTY WHO KNOWS THE ANSWER. I believe if the question was asked then, GOD will answer this question for me and you, my friends. This is a puzzling question that the only person that can answer this is JESUS CHRIST HIM SELF. Sometimes when we think that we are doing the right thing in the sight of man it becomes the wrong thing in the sight of JESUS CHRIST AND HIS HOLY FATHER. There is no doubt that many believers will go to Heaven, and some will end up in hell for minute things.

Several people will debate that it is exceptionally narrow-minded of GOD to provide single one way to heaven. Nonetheless, honestly, considering mankind's insurrection against GOD, it is very broad-minded for HIM to provide us with one way to Heaven. We deserve conviction, but GOD offers us the way of escape by sending HIS one-and-only SON to die for our sins. Whether somebody sees this as narrow or wide, it is the fact. The good news is that JESUS died and rose again; individuals who are going to Heaven have received this gospel by faith and kept their faith. To GOD be all the glory, today, Acts of Apostle 4:12 is not politically correct. Nowadays it is widespread to say, "Everybody's going to Heaven" or "All road leads to Heaven." Many of us today think we can make Heaven without surrendering our life to JESUS. We want the glory, but we do not want to be bothered by the cross, much less the LORD JESUS who died there. Several people do not want to accept JESUS as the only way of going to Heaven and they decided to find alternative pathway. But JESUS warns us that no other path exists and that the result for rejecting this truth is an eternity in hell. HE told us that "whoever believes in the Son has eternal life, but whoever rejects the Son will not see life, for God's wrath remains on him" (John 3:36). FAITH IN CHRIST JESUS IS THE FUNDAMENTAL TO GOING TO HEAVEN.

> **Be incredibly careful, then, how you live –not as unwise but as wise (Ephesians 5:15)**

No body can tell who qualify to enter GOD'S kingdom? How can we ensure that we are going to HEAVEN? The Bible makes a clear difference between those who have eternal life and those who do not: "He who has the Son has life; he who does not have the Son of God does not have life" (1 John 5:12). The situation goes back to faith. Individuals who believe in Christ are made the children of God (John 1:12). Those who accept Jesus' sacrifice as the payment for their sins and who believe in His resurrection are going to heaven. Those who reject

Christ are not. "Whoever believes in him is not condemned, but whoever does not believe stands condemned already because he has not believed in the name of God's one and only Son" (John 3:18). Several individuals today hold to a weakened gospel that does away with the need for repentance. They want to believe in a "loving" God who never references sin and who requires no switch in their lifestyle. They might say stuffs like, "My GOD would not ever send a person to hell." However, JESUS talked more about hell than HE did about Heaven, and HE exhibited HIMSELF as the SAVIOR who presents the only ways of going to Heaven: "I am the way, the truth, and the life. No one comes to the Father except through me" (John 14:6).

According to the WORD OF JESUS CHRIST, "MANY ARE CALLED, BUT FEW ARE CHOSEN." (Matthew 22:14). It is only the WORD OF GOD that will enlighten us on the standard of who qualify to go to Heaven? As amazing as Heaven will be for those who accept JESUS CHRIST as their SAVIOR, hell will be WORST for those who reject JESUS. Individual cannot read the Bible genuinely without seeing it repeatedly—the line is drawn. The Bible says there is one and only one way to heaven—JESUS CHRIST. Follow JESUS' command: "Enter through the narrow gate. For wide is the gate and broad is the road that leads to destruction, and many enter through it. But small is the gate and narrow the road that leads to life, and only a few find it" (Matthew 7:13-14). Belief in JESUS is the only way of going to Heaven. Those who have faith are assured to enter Kingdom of GOD. Have you given your life to JESUS? It is not late. If you are already a believer, Are you faithfully and honestly following JESUS WHOLEHEATEDLY?

Not All Who Claim To Be Believers In CHRIST Will Go To HEAVEN!

Sin must be punished, or else God is not just (2 Thessalonians 1:6). Brothers and sisters, the verdict we face at death is simply GOD passing on our accounts up to date and bringing sentence on our criminalities against HIM. We have no way to make our crimes right. Our good does not offset our bad. One sin ruins faultlessness, just as one droplet of arsenic in a tumbler of water destroys the entire glass. So, GOD became man and took our penalty upon Him. Jesus was GOD in the flesh. He lived a sinless life of obedience to His Father (Hebrews 4:15). HE had no sin, yet at the cross HE took our sin and made it HIS own. Once He paid the price for our sin, we could be declared holy and perfect (2 Corinthians 5:21).

When we confess our sin to Him and ask His forgiveness, He stamps "Paid in Full" over our life of selfishness, lust, and greed (Acts 2:38; 3:19; 1 Peter 3:18). Our LORD JESUS SAID it IN HIS WORDS: "Not everyone who calls out to me, 'Lord! Lord!' will enter the Kingdom of Heaven. Only those who do the will of my Father in heaven will enter. 22 On judgment day many will say to me, Lord! Lord! We prophesied in your name and cast out demons in your name and performed many miracles in your name.' 23 But I will reply, I never knew you. Get away from me, you who break God's laws" (Matthew 7:21-23).

{
**Finally, my brethren, be strong in the
Lord and in the power of His might
(Ephesians 6:10)**
}

Brothers and sisters in CHRIST, we are aware of what the Scripture said in John 3:16. The truth is that the Scripture has much to say about life after death, and it has become a challenge to public opinion. John 3:16 says, "For God so loved the world that he gave his one and only Son, that whoever believes in him shall not perish but have eternal life." At the time, in verse thirty-six, JESUS goes on to say, "Whoever believes in the SON has eternal life, but whoever rejects the Son will not see life, for God's wrath remains on them." Hebrews 9:27 says, "It is appointed to men once to die, but after this the judgment." According to these verses, everyone dies, but not everyone goes to heaven (Matthew 25:46; Romans 6:23; Luke 12:5; Mark 9:43). GOD is HOLY and perfect. Heaven, His dwelling place, is holy and perfect, too (Psalm 68:5; Nehemiah 1:5; Revelation 11:19). According to Romans 3:10, "there is none righteous, no not one." No human being is holy and perfect enough for heaven.

Unbelievably, the people we call "good" are not good enough to compare to the sinless perfection of GOD. If GOD allowed sinful humans to enter the perfection of HEAVEN, it would no longer be perfect. What standard should be used to determine who is "good enough?" GOD'S standard is the only one that counts, and HE has already ruled. Romans 3:23 says that "all have sinned and fallen short of God's glory." And the payment for that sin is eternal separation from God (Romans 6:23). Self-righteousness will not take anyone one of us to HEAVEN.

What Should We Do To Go To HEAVEN?

We must not be deceiving ourselves. The Scripture is clear on what we can do to inherit the KINGDOM of GOD. It is for you and me to follow the right path and escape from eternal deamination. GOD sent HIS SON to reconcile us to HIMSELVE. JESUS came to this wicked world to redeem us. He was born as a poor child. He died as a criminal. He defeated Satan and rose as a Hero. HE came back to life with the key to death and life. HE ascended to HEAVEN and was sitting now on the right HAND OF HIS FATHER. HE is coming back to rule and to reign in the entire world. HE will be the KING OF ALL KINGS AND THE LORD OF ALL LORDS. What then is the way to HEAVEN? "The only way to HEAVEN is through JESUS CHRIST and JESUS CHRIST ALONE. Our LORD JESUS CHRIST is HIMSELF the way to HEAVEN. HE does not merely show the way; HE IS THE WAY. Salvation is only in the person of Jesus Christ" (John14:6). How to Prepare for HEAVEN While on Earth: Since HEAVEN is our future endpoint, how can we prepare on earth for living there? This is a good question. The answer is in the Bible. Receive Jesus Christ as your Savior.

Things We Must Do To Make HEAVEN!

1. **Avoid the work of fresh**

   Flesh and Spirit are always at war. Walking in the Spirit is of the LORD, while walking in the flesh is the devil. The work of the flesh is one of the things that will make us not go to HEAVEN. This can be disturbing for each of us because most of the time, the easiest thing to do is to follow our sinful flesh than the leadership of the HOLY SPIRIT. Obeying the HOLY SPIRIT and following HIM is always the right thing to do. Letting ourselves to be led by THE HOLY SPIRIT will help us grow in our affiliation in CHRIST. In addition, it will also help us grow in our Christian race. When we select to follow the sinful flesh, we are disobeying or disappointing GOD, others, and ourselves. Following the lead of the HOLY SPIRIT can be hard, but it is worth it. I am a living testimony on follow the lead of the HOLY SPIRIT. It is significant to note that if we are not being directed by the HOLY SPIRIT, then we are being led by our own sinful nature. The walk of the Spirit is stretched out in the Book of Galatians (5:16-21). I believe this portion of the Scripture should be our yard stick to make sure we are on the right track in serving and walking with our MAKER.

{
Be incredibly careful, then, how you live –not as unwise but as wise (Ephesians 5:15)
}

2. **Living By the Spirit Power**

The works of flesh will always produce sin. As believers, we should as much as run away from work of flesh. To allow the HOLY SPIRIT to lead us, we must follow HIS guidance. In addition to yielding to HIS opinion, we can also become aware of the HOLY SPIRIT'S leading through reading the Bible.

So I say, let the Holy Spirit guide your lives. Then you will not be doing what your sinful nature craves. The sinful nature wants to do evil, which is just the opposite of what the Spirit wants. And Spirit gives us desires that are the opposite of what the sinful nature desires. These two forces are constantly fighting each other, so you are not free to conduct your good intentions. But when the Spirit directs you, you are not under obligation to the law of Moses. When you follow the desires of your sinful nature, the results are noticeably clear: sexual immorality, impurity, lustful pleasures, idolatry, sorcery, hostility, quarreling, jealousy, outbursts of anger, selfish ambition, dissension, division, envy, drunkenness, wild parties, and other sins like these. Let me tell you again, as I have before, that anyone living that sort of life will not inherit the Kingdom of God (Galatians 5:16-21).

3. **Follow The Leadership of The HOLY SPIRIT:**

There is much information about the HOLY SPIRIT in the Bible and the more we study about HIM, the healthier we will be at discerning HIS leading and guidance. A few aspects of the HOLY SPIRIT'S leading are the fruits of the Spirit. (Galatians 5:22-23) states, "But the fruit of the Spirit is love, joy, peace, forbearance, kindness, goodness, faithfulness, gentleness, and self-control. Against such things there is no law." These fruits of the Spirit are what God wants to promote in our lives. When the SPIRIT is leading us, we will harvest these fruits in our lives, as well as love, joy, peace, forbearance, kindness, goodness, faithfulness, gentleness, and self-control.

4. **Live A Holy Life**

Brothers and sisters in CHRIST, we must aspire to live a holy life for GOD. GOD is Holy and we must be holy unto HIM. "But as he which hath called you is holy, so be ye holy in all manner of conversation; Because it is written, be ye holy; for I am holy" (1st Peter 1:15-16). It is important for us to be aware of our environment. We should be able to ask the HOLY SPIRIT of GOD to help us to be able to read the handwriting on the wall. According to the Gospel of Luke, we were encouraged to be alert and not be careless with our Christian race. "But watch yourselves lest your hearts be weighed down with dissipation and drunkenness and cares of this life, and that day come upon you suddenly like a trap." (Luke 21:34). The question of what to do to enter Heaven is very crucial in our lives as Believers. I believe the first thing we need to do is to run away from loss of flesh. Spirit and flesh do not go together. You must have faith in the TRINITY, GOD THE FATHER, GOD THE SON AND GOD THE HOLY SPIRIT. "By faith Noah, being warned by God concerning events yet unseen, in reverent fear constructed an ark for the saving of his household. By this he condemned the world and became an heir of the righteousness that comes by faith" (Hebrews 11:7).

> **Be incredibly careful, then, how you live –not as unwise but as wise (Ephesians 5:15)**

5. Have Faith In GOD

Brethren, as followers of CHRIST, we all are encouraged to have faith in GOD, but then again what precisely does that mean? In what way are we to increase our faith in HIM? To have faith in GOD I believe means to have faith in IN HIM. This means we should understand HIS personality and know HE will not ask us what we cannot do; whatever HE permits to happen will be done for our benefit. Our father Abraham had faith in GOD, and it was counted to him as righteousness. As sons and daughters of Abraham, we should also follow his footsteps in having faith and obeying GOD in every areas of our life. "Then Jesus said to the disciples, "Have faith in GOD. I tell you the truth, you can say to this mountain, 'May you be lifted up and thrown into the sea,' and it will happen. But you must really believe it will happen and have no doubt in your heart" (Mark 11:22-24). In every Believers life, faith has the influence to move the hand of GOD. I want to make myself clear here, none of us could manipulate GOD or force HIM do anything HE does not want to do. But faith moves GOD'S power to change in our lives. "For in it the righteousness of God is revealed from faith for faith, as it is written, "The righteous shall live by faith" (Romans 1:17).

The Bible clearly stated that this happen more than a few times during JESUS' ministry in answer to a person's faith, they were healed or granted a request they had asked for. Let us not kid ourselves there are periods when it is hard to have faith in God. When life gets problematic, it is enticing to give in to the cries of the world and hesitation that GOD is good. You may even begin to be certain that you have lost your faith. "And without faith it is impossible to please him, for whoever would draw near to God must believe that he exists and that he rewards those who seek him" (Hebrews 11:6). OH' LORD Is not that breathtaking? When we confess to have faith in GOD, it goes outside a simple trust. We are calling upon who HE is and bringing ourselves into line with HIM. Faith pleases GOD. Not only does HE want us to believe that HE exists, BUT HE ALSO wants us to know HE will reward those who remain faithful to HIM.

6. Obedience To GOD

Let us ask ourselves these simple questions? What are my spiritual benefits in obeying GOD? What is the importance of obedience? Obedience is so important for every Christ follower, in fact without it, we will fall short of GOD'S GLORY and HIS expectation of us. Obedience it is a performance of worship as it proves our love for GOD and sets us apart. Obedience is the hallmark of our salvation. Even though we are saved by Grace through the redeeming work of the Cross and by the BLOOD OF JESUS; It is our obedience that sets us apart as faithful children of GOD.

There is no doubt that obedience is our way to show GOD that HE is loved by us; and it is through our obedience that GOD recognizes us and enables us to enjoy HIS Love. Therefore, our main reason for obedience must be to demonstrate to GOD that we love HIM. This in turn will allow GOD to reveal HIMSELF to us and activates GOD'S power to work in our lives.

> **Be careful, then, how you live –not**
> **as unwise but as wise**
> **(Ephesians 5:15)**

7.   **Rewards For Fearing GOD!**

From time to time, even when we know the things that GOD expects from us, acting on them will not be easy for us. Numerous times, obedience means sacrifice; every now and then obedience can be painful; sometimes it can mean stretching ourselves outside our comfort Precinct. On our own we may not be able to do it. We therefore need GOD'S help through the HOLY SPIRIT to help us. We remember what happened in the Garden of Gethsemane: When JESUS was tired and stressed out. The Human side of HIM wanted to give up, at point, HE even prayed if HIS FATHER could take away the cup from HIM but remembered to say, "Not my will but your will."

There are rewards in obedience to GOD:

- We will be favored and blessed wherever we go.

- Our children will be blessed.

- God will protect us.
  Everything we set our firsthand will be fruitful.

- The LORD will help us to stand firm.

You can make this choice by loving the LORD your GOD, obeying HIM, and committing yourself firmly to HIM. **THIS IS THE KEY TO YOUR LIFE.** And if you love and obey the LORD, you will live long in the land the LORD swore to give your ancestors Abraham, Isaac, and Jacob." (Deuteronomy 30:20). "Love the LORD your GOD, walk in all HIS ways, obey HIS commands, hold firmly to HIM, and serve HIM with all your heart and all your soul" (Joshua 22:5). Jesus replied, "All who love me will do what I say. My Father will love them, and we will come and make our home with each of them" (John 14:23). "But do not just listen to GOD'S word. You must do what it says. Otherwise, you are only fooling yourselves" (James 1:22). "Do not copy the behavior and customs of this world, but let God transform you into a new person by changing the way you think. Then you will learn to know God's will for you, which is good, pleasing, and perfect" (Romans 12:2). We need to completely forsake sin and follow JESUS. CHRIST SAID

8.   **GO AND SIN NO MORE!**

JESUS said to sinners: "Go and sin no more." Our SAVIOR still called out their sin. HE did not leave them in their sin. He challenged them just as HE challenged the religious rulers, just in a dissimilar way because their mindset and hearts were not the same. But it does not mean that we do not say truth and the truth is that there are a lot of persons who use the title "Believers" who have not ever had a personal encounter with CHRIST. If we do not discourse this, we leave them in their lost state and do them no favors. I would rather somebody upset me with this fact than leave me on a pathway to everlasting destruction.

{
**Be very careful, then, how you
live –not as unwise but as wise
(Ephesians 5:15)**
}

CHAPTER 1

THE LAMB MARRIAGE SUPPER

Who Were the First Invitees to Marriage Supper?

According to history the Jewish people were first to be invited for the marriage supper. Those people who were called by GOD'S servants for example, HIS Prophets down to John the Baptist to get themselves ready by preparing for the coming of the MESSIAH. They did not obey the call; for a kingdom, the situation of belonging to which was self-punishment, did not please them. The original guests invited were the Jews. The Jews thought that since they were GOD'S chosen people that was all that was obligatory to go into the Kingdom of HEAVEN (for example to be invited to the wedding banquet.

Are You Ready for The Marriage Invitation?

He ordered the servants to bind this man and to throw him into the darkness where he will cry and gnash his teeth. The inappropriately dressed man characterizes those who were not ready for complete obligation to JESUS. Each time we partake in HOLY COMMUNION as instructed by JESUS, we are invited into the marriage supper of the LAMB, the HEAVENLY feast, the spiritual wedding banquet of the LAMB declared in the book of Revelation.

Who Is Qualified To Be At The Marriage Super Invitation?

For sure anyone who is living a sinful life will not be invited to this Marriage Supper. The class of people that will be at the Marriage Supper are those who served the LORD and followed HIM to the end. The bride class are those who are faithful to the LORD in every part of their lives for they trail the LAMB wherever HE leads (Revelation 14:3,4). They keep themselves unblemished from all GOD'S creatures, keep their ceremonial dress spotless and short of crease, rejoice in tribulation (Romans 5:3) "Count it all joy to suffer with and for the body of Christ" (Colossians 1:24). These are the ones who take extra oil (Holy Spirit) for their vessels (Matthew 25:4) to endure the testing's Comprised are those whose endurance and ideas are not dark. Likewise, those who do not get preoccupied and lose focus totally before the bridegroom comes, individuals whose holiness is not contaminated, and their clothing not blemished and those whose dress is righteous in addition continuously accurate on time. Those who washed their clothes in the blood of the LAMB.

> **For many are called, but few are chosen**
> **(Matthew 22:14)**

The Orientation to the Marriage Supper of the Lamb:

In a new job, we are required to be properly oriented to our new job so we can adequately familiarize ourselves with the expectations of the organization. Without orientation, the company will not hold you accountable for performing less than expected. If you make a mistake the leadership of your company will not terminate your appointment because that management failed to provide you with proper orientation. In Nursing field, orientation is provided for 8 to 12 weeks before a new RN will be assigned to take care of a patient. We have all been properly oriented as per what we need to attend the marriage supper of the LAMB. In the Book of Revelation 21:8 gave us a detailed orientation. "But the cowardly, unbelieving, abominable, murderers, sexually immoral, sorcerers, idolaters, and all liars shall have their part in the lake which burns with fire and brimstone, which is the second death" (Revelation 21:8 NKJV). Included are those whose patience and visions are not darkened. Also, those who do not get distracted and lose focus completely before the bridegroom comes, those whose holiness is not polluted, and their garment not stained and those whose garment is righteous and always right on time.

In Revelation 19:7 John recorded part of the loud proclamation of a great multitude in Heaven (vv. 1, 6): "Let us be glad and rejoice and give honor to him; for the marriage of the Lamb is come, and his wife hath made herself ready." Concerning the wife of the Lamb, John continued to write, "And to her was granted that she should be arrayed in fine linen, clean and white; for the fine linen is the righteousnesses of saints. And he saith unto me, Write, Blessed are they who are called unto the marriage supper of the Lamb" (vv. 8–9). Several things presented in the Book of the Revelation indicate that the Church will be in Heaven with Christ during that period. One of those things is the marriage and marriage supper of the Lamb.

Who Will Not Be Invited To The Marriage Supper?

Brothers and sisters in CHRIST unfortunately, sinners will not be invited to the marriage Supper of the LAMB. Time to mend our ways to do the right thing before GOD is running out! CHRIST can come at any time. We are already at end time. CHRIST JESUS is coming back to judge the world. HE will rule the entire world. Is the LORD JESUS your anchor that will faithfully keep your soul? Everything that is happening around us is leading to the return of the LORD JESUS CHRIST THE MESSIAH. In the heart of every true believer is the assurance that JESUS CHRIST will come back to earth and deal with those who living a sinful life. The BRIDE of CHRIST is made up of overcoming saints who have "washed their robes and made them white in the blood of the Lamb." What is the significance of the white wedding apparel of the Lamb's wife as indicated in the following Scriptures? It is imperative for all of us believers to guide ourselves to a realization that if we are to be part of the Bride of CHRIST it becomes necessary the attributes Apostle Paul wrote down for us to follow: 2nd Corinthians 11:2; We need to guide ourselves to an understanding that if we are to be a part of the BRIDE of CHRIST it will be necessary to possess these attributes; "For I am a jealous for you with godly jealousy. For I have betrothed you to one husband, that I may present you as a chaste virgin to Christ" (2nd Corinthians 11:2; NKV).

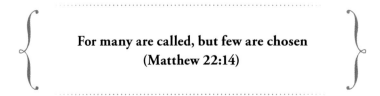

For many are called, but few are chosen
(Matthew 22:14)

Conditions For The Marriage Supper of the Lamb!

In Revelation 19:7, the Apostle John the beloved recorded part of the loud declaration of a great multitude in Heaven (vv. 1, 6): "Let us be glad and rejoice and give honor to him; for the marriage of the Lamb comes, and his wife hath made herself ready." Concerning the wife of the Lamb, John continued to write, "And to her was granted that she should be arrayed in fine linen, clean and white; for the fine linen is the righteousnesses of saints. And he saith unto me, Write, Blessed are they who are called unto the marriage supper of the Lamb" (vv. 8–9).

The Parable of The Wedding Feast

The parable of the wedding feast is a parable about multiplicity. Jesus teaches that the Kingdom of God is open to everyone, not only Jews. This is where JESUS said, "Many are invited, but few are chosen." This parable was told using the conversational setting of a wedding feast, however, there are a few surprising events included. According to the Scripture, a king was fixing a wedding feast for his son. He sent his servants out to bring the requested guests, but they did not care about the invitation. They refused to honor the invitation and refused to come. The servants were once again, sent out with the message, "Look, I have prepared my dinner, my oxen and my fat calves have been slaughtered, and everything is ready; come to the wedding banquet." In this scenario, the king was somehow disappointed that his invitees did not want to come despite him been a king. Some people overlooked the servants and went as an alternative to their businesses. Some of them seized the servants, abused them, and then killed them. The king became violent and sent troops to destroy the killers and burn their city. He then instructed his servants to invite anyone they found, so that both good and bad people filled the hall at the marriage ceremony banquet. Their reactions were very strange and severe.

Here that GOD is the one inviting everyone of to come to HIS SONS wedding feast. How did we react to this glorious invitation? We rejected or refused the invitation. May the LORD help us to attend the wedding ceremony of GODS SON? Friends, let us ask ourselves this question? Is our reaction not even worse today? Every one of us has been divinely invited to this glorious marriage supper. How do we as individuals or as the entire universe respond to this invitation? We need to be careful there is a day of judgement coming when each one of us will stand before GOD and the video will be played to show us how we spent our live here on earth. The Jews who disregarded the servants were those who overlooked the Prophets who came to deliver the message of GOD, and those who refused to believe in JESUS CHRIST. Those Jewish people who responded aggressively might be a reference to those who abused as well as murdered the Prophets and messengers of GOD and predicted of the rejection of JESUS CHRIST. The people who were invited subsequently are the Gentiles. This parable shows that the Kingdom of GOD is open to everyone, not just the Jews. At the end of this parable, we see communication among the king and a man who was not appropriately dressed up.

Compliance through trials will demonstrate whether they will be of the bride class or not. "Blessed are those who are invited to the marriage supper of the Lamb." (Revelation 19:9). The truth becomes if Christians are the bride, then who are the peoples? All through the gospel age, two classes are being developed that will receive a spirit resurrection in HEAVEN. The first is the intended class, also denoted to as "the little flock," "the straightforward," "the chosen, and faithful," "the wise virgins," "the body of Christ," "the spiritual house," and "144,000." (Revelation 21:9; Revelation 17:14; Matthew 25:8-10; Ephesians 1:22, 23; I Peter 2:5; Revelation 7:4) The other class, those less faithful Christians, is referred to as "the bride's companion," "the foolish virgins," "the tribulation saints," "the great multitude," (Psalms 45:14; Matthew 25:2; Revelation 7).

{
For many are called, but few are chosen
(Matthew 22:14)
}

Another class are those who do not show faith, and therefore do not qualify for the bride class. To them, life was a great tribulation. And I said to him, "Sir, you know." "So, he said to me, "These are the ones who come out of the great tribulation, and washed their robes and made them white in the blood of the Lamb" (Revelation 7:14). Their robes turn out to be soiled with the cares and untrustworthiness of materials of this world (Mark 4:19, Ephesians 5:27). When it comes time for the marriage to the bridegroom, they are found lacking. But because they are virgins and companions of the bride, they do get invited to the marriage supper (invitees). "The king's daughter is all glorious within: her clothing is of wrought gold. She shall be brought to the king in raiment of needlework: the virgins her companions that follow her shall be brought into thee. With gladness and rejoicing they shall be brought; They shall enter the King's palace" (Psalms 45:13-15). This portion of the Scripture says a volume about those who will be qualified for the marriage supper.

In the previous verses, the bride is observed corporately, on the edge of marrying the Lamb. Nonetheless, in Revelation 19: 7-9; 7 Let us be glad and rejoice and give Him glory, for the marriage of the Lamb has come, and His wife has made herself ready." 8 And to her it was granted to be arrayed in fine linen, clean and bright, for the fine linen is the righteous acts of the saints. 9 Then he said to me, "Write: 'Blessed are those who are called to the marriage supper of the Lamb!'" And he said to me, "These are the true sayings of God" (Revelation 19: 7-9 NKJV). It is obvious that this marriage supper of the Lamb would take place at Christ's Father's banquet hall in HEAVEN. It is not going to be at any of the five-star hotel banquet halls on earth. God already has the records of the invitees to the wedding feast of the LAMB. The focus is on individual believers who are represented as requested people at the marriage supper. In this vision that God gave to the apostle John, we are invited to take in the glory of "the bride, the wife of the Lamb." The glorified church is the bride of Christ (see Revelation 19:5).

{ **For many are called, but few are chosen (Matthew 22:14)** }

CHAPTER 2

KINGDOM OF GOD REQUIREMENTS

Friends, can we just tell ourselves the truth? There are standard rules and regulations for those who want to be admitted into the KINGDOM of GOD. GOD loved humankind hence HE sent HIS ONLY SON to die for us. HE watched HIS HOLY SON die a humiliating death on the Cross. CHRIST came to redeem us from the hands of satan. HE shed HIS OWN BLOOD so that we might have eternal life. The choice is ours now. This is the hour and time to make the decision if we want to be graciously gained admission to the KINGDOM of GOD. We are to keep the laws and commandments of GOD if we want to spend eternity with CHRIST. Unwise individuals will not inherit the KINGDOM of HEAVEN. GOD is not mocked anything that we sow, that we will reap. We cannot sow oranges and reap mangoes. Nature itself is against that.

The blood that JESUS shed is for all of us. We are required to love GOD with of all our heart, all our soul and all our strength. "For he has rescued us from the kingdom of darkness and transferred us into the Kingdom of his dear Son, who purchased our freedom and forgave our sins" (Colossians 1:13-14). Anything less than this is unqualified to be in the KINGDOM of GOD. The Scriptures tells us that "Not everyone who calls out to me, 'Lord! Lord!' will enter the Kingdom of Heaven. Only those who do the will of my Father in heaven will enter. ²²On judgment day many will say to me, Lord! Lord! We prophesied in your name and cast out demons in your name and performed many miracles in your name.' ²³But I will reply, I never knew you. Get away from me, you who break God's laws" (Matthew 7:21-23).

Brethren, one of the utmost experiences of life is to be among CHRIST followers. Each one of us has the responsibility of getting ourselves and others ready for entering the Kingdom of GOD on the last days of our life spending eternity with the LORD JESUS. The atoning sacrifice of our LORD made it possible for all humanity to be resurrected and to be raised up to immortality. GOD gave humanity resurrection and immortality. This is the greatest gift ever given. The apostle Paul put it this way: "For as in Adam all die, even so in Christ shall all be made alive." (1 Cor. 15:22). But to be resurrected and immortal is not all that is required for entering eternal life in the kingdom of GOD.

Everlasting life in the kingdom of GOD is far-off beyond HIS worldwide gift of immortality and is GOD'S greatest gift to all human beings; this will only happen through obedience to the doctrines in addition to commandments imparted by JESUS CHRIST. Again, Jesus said, "I am the way, the truth and the life: no man cometh unto the Father, but by me." (John 14:6).

> **Jesus replied, "I assure you; no one can enter the Kingdom of God without being born of water and the Spirit" (John 3:5)**

CHRIST said, "No man cometh unto the FATHER, but by me." This is the LORD'S way, and coming unto the FATHER is a divine and consecrated gift that must be deserved. "Seek the Kingdom of God above all else, and live righteously, and he will give you everything you need" (Matthew 6:33). The truth is that GOD'S utmost gift and blessing to HIS children is everlasting life with HIM in HIS HEAVENLY KINGDOM.

Nowadays, there is a lot of disagreement and argument among the doctrines and ideas of men and women comparative to the requirements for entering the kingdom of GOD. I believe this should not be since Scripture laid out everything for us. We need to pray that the HOLY SPIRIT OF GOD should open our eyes of understanding to grasp what the Bible is saying to us concerning this issue. Several of us have been misled by the educations of men. Those who works in disobedience to GOD'S mandates; they feel that they are not important, and even though some base their argument on scriptures. For instance, According to Apostle Paul's write up, he said that "For by grace are ye saved through faith; and that not of yourselves: it is the gift of God: Not of works, lest any man should boast." (Eph. 2:8–9). This is so true because none of us can say that we work so hard and that was why we had salvation. Our salvation is only the grace and mercy of GOD ALMIGHTY. The resurrection and the ability to live forever are gifts from GOD, through JESUS CHRIST, and not from the works and labors of earthly men.

A lot of us today including the so-called believers try to justify our claims with what JESUS said to the thief on the cross, when the thief said to Jesus, "Lord, remember me when thou comest into thy kingdom," and Jesus said unto him, "Verily I say unto thee, to day shalt thou be with me in paradise." (Luke 23:42–43). The LORD JESUS and the thief went to paradise. There are those who teach that paradise and heaven are the same place, but this is not according to the teachings of the Holy Scriptures. After human death, his or her spirit goes to paradise and remains there until the chosen period for its resurrection into immortality and eternal life.

HEAVEN, which is the KINGDOM OF GOD, is where those who have been obedient to GOD'S plan of life and salvation go after judgment and the resurrection. No sinner will go to HEAVEN. The only fuel to HEAVEN is strictly observing and maintaining the Commandments of GOD. After the death of JESUS CHRIST, HIS SPIRIT went to paradise and not to the KINGDOM OF HEAVEN. It was only after HIS resurrection that HE mentioned returning to the KINGDOM OF HEAVEN. Remember what HE told Mary as she stood by the sepulcher weeping: "Touch me not, for I am not yet ascended to my Father: but go to my brethren, and say unto them, I ascend unto my Father, and your Father; and to my God, and your God." (John 20:17). HIS SPIRIT had been to paradise, but HE had not yet ascended to HIS FATHER IN HEAVEN.

Friends, let us not kid ourselves we need to be always faithful to GOD. When Apostle Paul was writing to the Hebrew brethren, he wrote: "Therefore, as the Holy Spirit says: "Today, if you will hear His voice, Do not harden your hearts as in the rebellion, In the day of trial in the wilderness, Where your fathers tested Me, tried Me, And saw My works forty years. Therefore, I was angry with that generation, and said, 'They always go astray in their heart, and they have not known My ways.' So, I swore in My wrath, 'They shall not enter My rest.'" Beware, brethren, lest there be in any of you an evil heart of unbelief in departing from the living God (Hebrews 3:7-12 NKJV). JESUS warned that not very many would find their way and prepare themselves to live in the kingdom of HEAVEN. HE said, "Enter ye in at the strait gate: Because strait is the gate, and narrow is the way, which leadeth unto life, and few there be that find it." (Matt. 7:13–14).

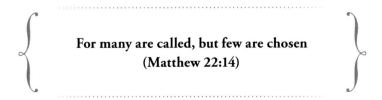

For many are called, but few are chosen (Matthew 22:14)

According to our LORD JESUS many will be misinformed and deceived by false teachers and false prophets, and some will desire to follow the ways of the world and will destroy their divine opportunity to enter the kingdom of HEAVEN. HE said, "Enter by the narrow gate; for wide is the gate and broad is the way that leads to destruction, and there are many who go in by it. Because narrow is the gate and difficult is the way which leads to life, and there are few who find it" (Matt. 7:13-14). JESUS encouraged us to pray to our FATHER IN HEAVEN. "But seek first the Kingdom of God and His righteousness, and all these things shall be added to you" (Matt. 6:33 NKJV).

There are some people who want a cheap and effortless way to heaven while continuing to live their own selfish and worldly lives on earth. We cannot serve two experts at the same time. If you are for CHRIST, be for HIM. Requirement for entering the KINGDOM of GOD one need to be fully and faithfully committed to keep the law of GOD. One of the Disciple of JESUS sates: that, "Not everyone who says to me, 'Lord, Lord,' will enter the kingdom of heaven, but only he who does the will of my Father who is in heaven." (Matthew 7:21). Jesus saves only those who fully trust in Him as Savior. The scriptures tell us, "Salvation is found in no one else, for there is no other name under heaven given to men by which we must be saved" (Acts 4:12).

When we hold tight to GOD, HE works HIS righteousness in us. "Do not copy the behavior and customs of this world, but let God transform you into a new person by changing the way you think. Then you will learn to know God's will for you, which is good, pleasing, and perfect" (Romans 12:2, NLT).

Finally, my brethren be strong in the Lord and in the power of His might. Put on the whole armor of God, that you may be able to stand against the wiles of the devil (Ephesians 6:10-11)

CHAPTER 3

MANY ARE CALLED

The WORD of JESUS that many are called but few are chosen was in process before Prophet Isaiah, and it has been in action for the meantime of Prophet Isaiah. That word of prophecy is the most repeated passage in all scripture. It is repeated more times than any other scripture in the bible. It is the scripture that the Lord used to call me to ministry: Matthew 13:13-16. In effect, GOD declares that; consequently, numerous persons will determine to hear the gospel, nonetheless they will not listen." Only an extremely limited number of people will be saved. The testament of JESUS is "the spirit of prophecy." (Revelation 19:10). As a result, no matter what any person thinks, comparatively insufficient Christians are going to end up in heaven through the grace of GOD only. As we walk in our Christian journey, our basic belief is that we recognize HOLY BIBLE as the WORD OF GOD.

THE BIBLE IS NOT AN ORDINARY BOOK. IT IS THE SWORD OF THE SPIRIT.

HOLY BIBLE: WE BELIEVE THE BIBLE IS INSPIRED AND AUTHORIZED BY GOD, DEPENDABLE ALSO AUTHORITATIVE.

TRINITY: WE BELIEVE IN ONE EVERLASTING GOD WHO EXISTS AS THREE DISTINCT PERSONS; GOD THE FATHER, GOD THE SON, AND GOD THE HOLY SPIRIT.

JESUS CHRIST: WE BELIEVE THAT HE IS THE SON OF GOD, BORN OF A VIRGIN, LIVED A SINLESS LIFE AS HE WALKED AMONG MEN, ESTABLISHED THE AUTHORITY AND SUPREMACY OF GOD IN THE WHOLE THING AND SPEECH, DIED ON THE CROSS AS A CRIMINAL.

ROSE FROM THE DEAD: ON THE THIRD DAY, IN ADDITION HE IS NOW SEATED AT THE RIGHT HAND OF GOD HAVING ACCOMPLISHED ALL THAT IS CRITICAL FOR MAN'S SALVATION. JESUS' DEMISE ON THE CROSS PERMITS ME AND YOU TO EMBRACE THE SOUL-CAPTIVATING FREEDOM OF ETERNITY THAT WE ARE INVITED TO SHARE IN AS CHRISTIANS.

REPENTANCE: WE BELIEVE IT IS ESSENTIAL FOR MAN/WOMEN TO REPENT OF THEIR SINS AND BY FAITH RECEIVE THE FINISHED WORK OF CHRIST BY CONFESSING HIM AS LORD AND SAVIOR WITH HIS MOUTH AND BELIEVING IN HIS HEART, RESULTING IN REGENERATION BY THE HOLY SPIRIT.

> **Be careful, then, how you live –not as unwise but as wise (Ephesians 5:15)**

According to the revelation of CHRIST who is the LORD GOD ALMIGHTY, "many are called, but few are chosen." (Matthew 22:14). Friends in CHRIST, this word of CHRIST scares me a lot. I am personally sensitive with this portion of the scripture written in RED BY JESUS CHRIST HIMSELF. The testimony of JESUS is "the spirit of prophecy." (Revelation 19:10). Consequently, no matter what anyone of us thinks, comparatively few Christians are going to end up in HEAVEN and some will end up in hell fire. May the LORD forbid that any one of us will end up in hell. Our HEAVENLY FATHER said that hell is meant for Satan and his agents. It is not the will of GOD that anyone should perish but that all should come to repentance. Yes, many are called, but few are going to be chosen. Few are going to spend eternity with GOD. HE who has an ear, let him hear what the SPIRIT has been saying to the churches. (Revelation 2:29).

From the first time the gospel was preached, the message has been the same, but people have refused to listen. Isaiah cried: "Who has believed our report?" People have simply refused to believe the report of the LORD. The word of prophecy that many are called but few are chosen was in operation before Isaiah and it has been in operation since Isaiah. That word of prophecy is the most repeated passage in all scripture. It is repeated more times than any other scripture in the bible. I strongly belief that this is the scripture that the LORD used to call most of us into ministry: Matthew 13:13-16. GOD says in effect: "So many people will hear the gospel, but they will not listen." Only a very few individuals will be saved.

When Isaiah offered and asked the LORD to send him to preach the gospel, the LORD gave him a strange assignment: HE said, "Go, and tell this people: 'Keep on hearing, but do not understand; keep on seeing, but do not perceive.' Make the heart of this people dull and their ears heavy and shut their eyes; lest they see with their eyes, and hear with their ears, and understand with their heart, and return and be healed." (Isaiah 5:9-10). Isaiah could not believe this kind of task. What is the point of asking me to preach to people when you know that they will not listen? Isaiah had come forward for a job without knowing its full details. Maybe if he had known, he would not have been so forward. So, he asked the LORD: "How long?" "For how long shall I preach to them, and they will not listen? But the LORD'S answer brought no reprieve: "Until the cities are laid waste and without inhabitant, the houses are without a man, the land is utterly desolate." (Isaiah 6:11). GOD prophesied, in effect, that we would not listen until the destruction decreed has been affected. This is a powerful portion of the scripture. We would not listen until we are destroyed. How can a man listen after he has been destroyed? He will only listen when he is beyond redemption. Then he will remember all the warnings he heard and ignored. He will remember all the scriptures he overlooked. He will remember all the ones he highlighted in his bible but failed to practice. He will remember reading this article of faith.

Many Are Called, But Few Are Chosen (Matthew 22:14).

In any sports event, be it a marathon, soccer, football or basketball, a team might start well but not necessarily going to be the winning individual or a team. JESUS is GOD HIMSELF so HE knows the future and what it holds. HIS death on the Cross was for everybody. Fortunately, we are the reason HE died. So, in this WORD of JESUS "Many are called but only few are chosen is something every believer should take seriously for the course of the race we are in. I pray that believers will not joke with this statement of our LORD. In the story that JESUS told the Pharisees, the rich man finally believed the gospel but, alas, only when he was already in the grave. He was then concerned that his relatives should know that hades are real and not just a figment of someone's imagination. So he pleaded with Abraham that Lazarus should be sent to warn them from the grave: "Then he said, 'I beg you therefore, father, that you would send him to my father's house, for I have five brothers, that he may testify to them, lest they also come to this place of torment.' Abraham said to him, 'They have Moses and the prophets; let them hear them.' And he said, 'No, Father Abraham; but if one goes to them from the dead, they will repent.' But he said to him, 'If they do not hear Moses and the prophets, neither will they be persuaded though one rise from the dead." (Luke 16:27-31).

{
**Put on the new self, created to be like
God in true righteousness and holiness
(Ephesians 4:24)**
}

So determined is the LORD that this prophecy of unbelief is fulfilled that when CHRIST came in the flesh, HE was often speaking in parables. HIS disciples wondered about this tendency. They asked HIM: "Why can't you speak plainly to the people?" JESUS told them: "I AM always speaking in parables because I do not want the people to understand what I AM saying. "But why does JESUS not want the people to understand? JESUS does not want them to understand because HEAVEN is not for everyone. HEAVEN is only for a select few" (Matthew 13:11-16).

For 120 years, Noah preached the gospel. The truth is that the gospel has always been rejected and will always be rejected. Noah was recognized as a righteous man. During his time, only eight people were saved from the Flood. Lot preached the gospel to the citizens of Sodom and Gomorrah, pleading with them to repent and live a righteous life but the refused. At last, only Lot and his two daughters were saved. Even his wife perished when she looked back to Sodom and Gomorrah against GOD'S own instructions. Moses one of the greatest prophets in the history of the Bible, also preached the gospel of salvation to children of Israel; Even though, that a varied multitude of over two million people that left Egypt with Moses, yet only two entered the Promised Land. GOD would have all men to be saved. (I Timothy 2:3-4). But alas, only a few will be saved.

Dear brothers and sisters in CHRIST, it does not matter if you are still burning for CHRIST or you have backslidden, find a way to make peace with JESUS CHRIST THE LORD AND SAVIOR before it is too late for you. It could be that in the Bible group that you belong, and you are well known as a fire brand for JESUS; but you are not in a right position with CHRIST; but you have drifted away from the LORD. Nonetheless, because of what people will say you refused to confess your sins to GOD or to your fellow believers because of pride or arrogance. Remember the LORD said that the first shall be the last; and the last shall be the first. There is time and room to make it right with HIM who sits on the THRONE OF MERCY. The prodigal son came back to his father and the earthly father welcomed him with wide open hand, how much more.

PRAYER:

Dear, ALL AND MIGHTY GOD, I realize that I have sinned and have broken divine relationship with you. I have now realized my foolishness and carelessness with my walk with my holy FATHER. YOUR MERCY ARE NEW EVERY MORNING. Just talk to your GRACIOUS FATHER; HE will welcome you with HIS HANDS WILD OPEN. Restoration and forgiveness will immediately take place. Let us pray my brothers and sisters. FATHER, please restore my relationship with YOU, JESUS, and the HOLY SPIRIT. YOUR SON JESUS died on the Cross, paid for my sins, and rose again to give me eternal life. Please forgive me for my sins. I believe in my heart and openly confess that JESUS CHRIST IS THE SON OF GOD. HE IS THE LORD of my life. I am a child of GOD. Thank you for receiving me as your child IJMN AMEN. Make your way back to HIM now. HE IS FAITHFUL TO FORGIVE YOU AND TAKE YOU AS HIS CHILD.

{ **Put on the new self, created to be like God in true righteousness and holiness (Ephesians 4:24)** }

SALVATION: JESUS CHRIST IS THE MESSIAH, REDEEMER, AND THE SAVIOR!

All of us believe that we are saved by grace through faith in JESUS CHRIST: HIS death, burial, and resurrection. Salvation is a gift from GOD, not a result of my or your good works or of any human efforts of brothers and sisters in CHRIST. HE is JESUS, i.e., THE SAVIOR: who as the SON of GOD ALMIGHTY became a sinless man in order that through HIS sacrificial death, HE might pay for the sins of the world and thereby reconcile us to GOD; and show us how to truly live more so those of us who call ourselves Christians. We suppose the light of the world. Light ought to outshine darkness. We cannot claim to be the followers of CHRIST and yet live in a sinful lifestyle. This is undoubtedly one of the most frequent questions an individual believer will ask; particularly when each one of us begins to realize how short this life is in addition to the fact that there is an eternity on the other side of it. In fact, the only one who could truthfully response to this question is GOD HIMSELF, since HE is the ONE who created us and time and HEAVEN.

HEAVEN OR HELL?

Majority of believers believe in the impending return of JESUS and that those who believed in HIM will be resurrected to a HEAVENLY house in an incorruptible body, and those who do not believe will join Satan and his host in everlasting punishment. JESUS' death on the cross allows us to embrace the soul-gripping liberty of eternity that we are invited to share in as believers. "But to all who believed him and accepted him, he gave the right to become children of God" (John 1:12). Humankind is born into a curse of sin we cannot control; nonetheless we serve an ALMIGHTY AND EVERLASTING GOD who has made a way for us to escape it by HIM sending HIS ONLY BEGOTTEN SON JESUS CHRIST OUR REDEEMER; This Scriptural promise promises that "every ear will have a chance to hear," and JESUS will not come back until then. Nevertheless, CHRIST will surely be back.

For those who have accepted HIM AS OUR SAVIOR, and live a life worthy of their calling, will get to stare into the face of Prince of Peace and embrace the KING OF ALL KINGS. "He will wipe every tear from their eyes, and there will be no more death or sorrow or crying or pain. All these things are gone forever" (Revelation 21:4). "Then, together with them, we who are still alive and remain on the earth will be caught up in the clouds to meet the Lord in the air. Then we will be with the Lord forever. (1 Thessalonians 4:17).

LIFE AFTER DEATH

I remember as a child, I get hysterical when death occurrence is announced in the village. I was more than scared. It was in 1990 when I was told of my father's demise that the idea of death became reality. I could not imagine in my heart that my father would one day die. As a believer, I have come to realize that death is inevitable. I was very upset that I was not around when my dad passed. The first thing I asked my older sister upon my arriving home was did my father give his life to CHRIST? She said yes. I was not sure because I now know that there is HEAVEN and hell. There was a time when we did not exist, but there will never be a time when we will not be. Death is inevitable, but it is not the end. Our eternal destiny waits for us few minutes after death. Let us come home. If we die today, where will we spend eternity? It does not matter whether you are a rich man or poor man; you must give account of how you spent your life here on earth.

> **Follow GOD'S example in everything you do because you are his dear children (Ephesians 5:1)**

In the Gospel of Luke 16:19-31, JESUS shares a parable that needs to scare everyone. The story here stresses the importance of settling our relationship with JESUS CHRIST on this side of death. First, JESUS points out the difference in two men's lives: one was wealthy, the other poor (Luke 16:19-21). They were not born into the same social classes. They were not in the same social hierarchies; one had much and the other had little or not. The LORD also spoke of the dissimilarity in their deaths. When the rich man and the poor died, they were both buried according to their culture. However, the LORD also shares the disparity of their eternities. "So it was that the beggar died and was carried by the angels to Abraham's bosom. The rich man also died and was buried.

And being in torments in Hades, he lifted his eyes and saw Abraham afar off, and Lazarus in his bosom" (Luke 16: 22-23). Also, CHRIST revealed the other side of death. The beggar was ushered to Heaven, while the rich man watched from Hell. Unfolding the glories of HEAVEN, JESUS shares that the poor man who once begged for crumbs was now seated at the highest place of honor. Adrian Rogers said that "HEAVEN is all that the all-beneficent loving heart of GOD would desire for you. HEAVEN is all that the OMNISCIENT mind of GOD could design for you. HEAVEN is all that the OMNIPOTENT hand of GOD could prepare for you." JESUS reveals Hell to be a place of sensory, emotional, and spiritual unhappiness; and because our spirits are eternal, the torments of Hell are eternal. (Luke 16:24-29.). But if we come to JESUS in repentance and faith, we can know, without any doubt, that HE will save us and keep us for all eternity.

{
**Be very careful, then, how you
live –not as unwise but as wise
(Ephesians 5:15)**
}

CHAPTER 4

A BELIEVER CAN MISS HEAVEN

What Could Prevent A Believer From Making Heaven?

Many people think they are saved when they are not. There is an earnest warning in this passage, and it is addressed to professing Christians. It is addressed to the Church (the Body of CHRIS) at Corinth and the warning is this: "Do not be deceived." Many think that they are going to Heaven, but they are going to hell. Several people in the Corinthians Church thought they were saved. They were living a careless lifestyle. In today's Christian Community, some have neutralized the Gospel of our LORD JESUS CHRIST to fit their narrative. They thought they were going to Heaven. Many church members today have the same problem (Matthew 7:21-23). Sin is the only thing that could prevent a believer from entering the Kingdom of GOD. Sin leads to death anywhere any time.

Many of us think that we are carnal Christians when in fact we are not Christians at all. If you go to church on Sunday but live like the devil the rest of the week, you are not saved. Some have even been taught the lie that if you are saved, you have eternal security and if you have eternal security, then it does not matter how you live, because you are going to go to Heaven anyway. You might well live like the devil. Paul would say that you are just deceiving yourself. The wicked will not inherit the kingdom. Just going to church, even regularly, and getting baptized will not save you. You cannot live any way you want and go to Heaven. That is not eternal security. It is antinomianism (is any view which rejects laws or legalism and argues against moral, religious, or social norms).

When you get saved, there is a change in your life. There must be a transformation in one's life. After giving this extensive list of sins, Paul says "and such were some of you." Some of the Corinthians lived like this before they became Christians. That is what some of them WERE (past tense) but they are no longer that. There are differences because at salvation three things happened. They were washed (which you need because sin makes you dirty and salvation makes you clean), sanctified (set apart to GOD positional) and justified. There are some BIG BUTS in this passage. Notice three in this one passage alone. And such were some of you: BUT ye are washed, BUT ye are sanctified, BUT ye are justified in the name of the LORD JESUS, and by the SPIRIT OF OUR GOD (I Corinthians 6:11 KJV). The KJV follows the Greek text here. You cannot separate religion from morality. As James says, faith without work is DEAD. If you are genuinely saved, there is going to be a change in your life. If you are different on the inside and you have been saved, you will not be the same on the outside.

{
**Be very careful, then, how you
live –not as unwise but as wise
(Ephesians 5:15)**
}

Not everyone will inherit the kingdom. The Bible teaches that some will enter the kingdom, and SOME WILL NOT. Some will possess the kingdom, and some will be EXCLUDED. Some will inherit the kingdom, and some will not. This challenges the doctrine of diversity. Universalism teaches that EVERYONE will one day be saved. The Bible teaches that God loves everyone. GOD loves the world (John 3:16).

The Bible also says that GOD does not want anyone to perish (I Timothy 2:3-4). It also teaches that many will perish. In fact, it says that MOST will perish (Matthew 7:13-14). Paul says that many people will get in. Not all will enter the kingdom of GOD. Even the worst sinners can be saved. Paul said, "such were some of you." Some of the members of the Corinthians Church were formerly gay people. Some were adulterers. Some worshiped idols but then they got saved. Paul does not say that all the Corinthians lived like this before they were saved. He does not even say that most of them did.

He said that some of them used to live like that. The message here is that GOD can save anyone murderers, crack heads, prostitutes, and drunkards. This displays the power of the Gospel. Real change is possible, but it has nothing to do with any individual. This contradicts the idea that "once gay always gay" or "once an alcoholic always an alcoholic." Some people believe that wicked people cannot inherit the Kingdom of GOD. If a wicked man repents from his or her wicked ways GOD is MECIFUL to forgive him or her. The truth is that the wicked can inherit the kingdom. Individuals who do not know the Scripture very well occasionally ask questions like; can GOD have saved murderers? Can GOD save gay people? Can GOD save prostitutes? The answer is that GOD can save every person who repents.

Everyone one of the ten sins listed in 1st Corinthians 6:9 can be forgiven and has been forgiven through the death of JESUS CHRIST. JESUS stated that all manner of sin can be forgiven (Matthew 12:31). The only sin that cannot be forgiven is when we blasphemy the HOLY SPIRIT OF GOD. Even the darkest sins that we can commit can be forgiven. The sin of sodomy can be forgiven. That was a sin so wicked that GOD wiped out the entire city but even the wicked sodomites could have their sins forgiven by GOD if they had repented and turned from their sins. The worst sin on the planet was CRUCIFYING CHRIST and the people who did this were told that if they had repented, they would be saved.

Do You Have To Be Sinless To Go To Heaven?

Paul does not say that you must be sinless to go to heaven. Sinless perfection is not possible. You do have to have all your sins forgiven to go to Heaven, but you do not have to live a sinless life to go to heaven. That is not even possible. Paul is not teaching salvation. The kingdom is not earned, it is inherited. An inheritance is something that you get when you die as a gift. It is not something that you work to receive. It is something that you get because you are part of the family. The Bible teaches that all believers are heirs (Ephesians 1: 14, 18; Colossians 1:12; 1 Peter 1:4; Acts 20:32); Romans 8:17 Titus 3:7)

Can A Christian Commit Any One Of These Sins?

Samson committed the sin of sexual immorality. He was visiting prostitutes, and he is the one who is listed in the great faith hall of fame in Hebrews 11. Ananias and Sapphira were guilty of greed. Apostle Paul did not say that a Christian cannot commit one of these sins. Who is there who has never had a covetous thought? A true believer could commit any one of these sins. There are examples in the Bible of believers committing some of these sins. David committed adultery. Solomon committed idolatry. He married all those pagan wives and started building temples to pagan gods because he loved his wives so much. Noah got drunk after the Flood. Christian can commit any sin and still go to Heaven, but a Christian cannot habitually live like any of these sinful lifestyles and still go to heaven. Christians must be sensitive to sin. GOD hates sin. Believers should run away from sin. Sin will lead to internal obliteration.

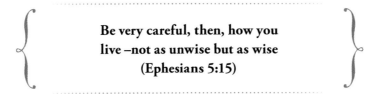

Be very careful, then, how you
live –not as unwise but as wise
(Ephesians 5:15)

14

Can One Be Gay, Lesbian or Transgender and Still Make Heaven?

YES, IF THEY REPENT! But if they do not repent, they will end up in hell. Our GOD is HOLY, so we need to be HOLY. "But at the beginning of creation GOD 'made them male and female" (Mark 10:6). No unholy person will go to Heaven. GOD'S eternal WORD reveals HIS plan for humankind and HIS intentions for marriage and sexuality. While Scripture teaches that same-gender acts are sinful, these Bible verses are not about condemning homosexuals, gays, lesbians, or transgender people. Rather, read GOD'S loving cautioning and offer of HIS grace for those who have wander away from HIS will for sex. We live in a fallen world with a fallen nature, but in CHRIST, we can be new creations. "'Do not have sexual relations with a man as one does with a woman; that is detestable. (Leviticus 18:22). Whether we like or not, homosexual lifestyle is a sin that will lead anyone that practices it will not inherit the Kingdom of GOD. It is an abomination to GOD. GOD loves individual that practices this, but HE hates the sin which eventually lead them to hell fire.

Although they know GOD'S righteous decree that those who do such things deserve death, they not only continue to do these very things but also approve of those who practice them (Romans 1:32). In the same way the men also abandoned natural relations with women and were inflamed with lust for one another. Men committed shameful acts with other men and received in themselves the due penalty for their error (Romans 1:27). "If a man has sexual relations with a man as one does with a woman, both have done what is detestable. They are to be put to death; their blood will be on their own heads" (Leviticus 20:13).

The question is not, what do people think about this question but what does the WORD OF GOD say about this? What does GOD say about this topic is what counts. The WORD OF GOD IS YES AND AMEN. It does not matter what the society say, it does not matter what law the government puts together about inclusiveness or approval of gay marriage or lesbian marriages. It is different from what contemporary psychology says. It is dissimilar from what the news media and entertainment industry say. GOD'S thoughts are not our thoughts (Isaiah 55:8-9). JESUS says, "What is highly esteemed among men is DETESTABLE in GOD'S sight" (Luke 16:15-16). Paul says in this passage that homosexuals will NOT enter the kingdom. These are not my words. I did not write them.

The WORD OF GOD says that they will NOT go to heaven. Paul does not say if people do these things, they will not get any rewards in heaven. He says that they will not be there. He also says that a lot of heterosexuals will NOT be there either. The Bible does NOT just single out homosexuals. Let us look at the Scripture in the Book of 1st Corinthians 6:9-11; 9 Or do you not know that wrongdoers will not inherit the kingdom of GOD? Do not be deceived: Neither the sexually immoral nor idolaters nor adulterers nor men who have sex with men ten nor thieves nor the greedy nor drunkards nor slanderers nor swindlers will inherit the kingdom of God. 11 And that is what some of you were. But you were washed, you were sanctified, you were justified in the name of the Lord Jesus Christ and by the Spirit of our God" (1 Corinthians 6:9-11).

> **Finally, my brethren, be strong in the Lord and in the power of His might (Ephesians 6:10)**

Can One Be Gay or Lesbian and Transgender Still Be A Christian?

I am not saying that Christians cannot fall into all types of sins, including sexual sins in addition to homosexual sins. Believers can fall into the sin of adultery and even murder. King David committed adultery and murder, but he repented. I am not talking about an individual who struggles with and falls into a specific sin but continues in that sin and even defends it and claims it is not even a sin and reinterprets the Scripture to justify their sin. They say that GOD made them that way and make the Bible to say what they want it to say. It is additional matter to claim to be a Christian and agrees to take the Bible as the inspired, AUTHORITATIVE WORD OF GOD nonetheless to live completely opposing to what it teaches and defend that behavior. The latter claim to believe the Bible but revise and reinterpret it, making it say something that it does not say. You cannot claim to be a Christian when the Bible condemns that lifestyle. A Christian adulterer, gossiper, a Christian with anger, bitterness, or a Christian drunkard is an unfaithful person.

{
**Make the most of every opportunity
for doing good in these evil days
(Ephesians 5:16)**
}

CHAPTER 5

HOLY SPIRIT TRANSFORMATION

It is the HOLY SPIRIT'S job to produce CHRIST-LIKE character in all of us. This process of changing us to be more like JESUS is called sanctification. We cannot reproduce the character of JESUS on our own or by our own strength. New Year's resolutions, willpower, and best intentions are not enough. The Bible says, "The LORD makes us more and more like HIM as we are changed into HIS glorious image." (2 Corinthians 3:18). Only the HOLY SPIRIT has the power to make the changes GOD wants to make in our lives. Philippians 2:13 says, GOD is working in us, giving us the desire and the power to do what pleases HIM. When we hear the phrase, "the power of the HOLY SPIRIT," many people think of miracles and intense emotions. But most of the time, the HOLY SPIRIT'S power is released in our lives in quiet, unassuming ways that you are not even aware of or feel. The HOLY SPIRIT often pushes us with a gentle murmur.

The likeness of CHRIST is not produced by imitation but by inhabitation. We allow CHRIST to live through us. "This is the secret: CHRIST lives in you." (Colossians 1:27). This happens in real life through the choices we make. We choose to do the right thing in situations and then trust GOD'S SPIRIT to give us his power, love, faith, and wisdom to do it. Since GOD'S SPIRIT lives inside of us, these things are always available for the asking. Today expect the GOD of suddenly to visit you! In the book of Acts we see how ordinary people were transformed by the HOLY SPIRIT into extraordinary vessels in the hands of GOD. Even today, GOD is looking for ordinary people whom HE can use by the power of the HOLY SPIRIT. Expect the GOD of suddenly to visit you as you allow the power of the HOLY SPIRIT to cover you totally! (Acts 16:25-26). The Person of the suddenly is the HOLY SPIRIT.

HOLY SPIRIT TRANSFORMS US IN VARIOUS WAYS:

The HOLY SPIRIT gives believers the power to live like JESUS and be bold witnesses for HIM. Of course, there are many ways HE goes about doing this, so we are going to talk about the most common ones. JESUS said in John 16:7 that it was to our benefit that HE would go away so we would receive the HOLY SPIRIT: "But in fact, it is best for you that I go away, because if I do not, the Advocate will not come. If I do go away, then I will send HIM to you." If Jesus said it is best for us that he goes away, and then it must be because there is something valuable about what the HOLY SPIRIT was coming to do. We have evidence in the Scripture; "But you will receive power when the HOLY SPIRIT comes upon you.

> Do not copy the behavior and customs of this world, but let God transform you into a new person by changing the way you think. Then you will learn to know God's will for you, which is good and pleasing and perfect (Romans 12:2)

And you will be my witnesses, telling people about me everywhere - in Jerusalem, throughout Judea, in Samaria, and to the ends of the earth" (Acts 1:8). From this Scripture, we can gather the initial perception of what the HOLY SPIRIT does in our life as believers. JESUS sends the then believers out as witnesses and gave them the power to do it efficiently. Pray In the Spirit and Become Spiritually Alert.

Let us explore more what the HOLY SPIRIT does in the lives of Believers. As mentioned earlier, there are many ways that the HOLY SPIRIT works in the lives of Christians, but they all share one mutual goal: to make us more like JESUS CHRIST. HE works in believers by renewing our minds to be like the mind of CHRIST. He does this by convicting us of sin and leading us to repentance. Through repentance, HE wipes out what was dirty in us and allows us to bear good fruit. As we allow HIM to continue nourishing that fruit, we grow to resemble JESUS more. Personally, I call the HOLY SPIRIT OF GOD, my COMFORTER, MY CEO, MY DIRECTOR, MY MANAGER, MY LEADER, MY GUIDE, AND MY ALL IN ALL. "But the fruit of the Spirit is love, joy, peace, patience, kindness, goodness, faithfulness, gentleness, self-control; against such things there is no law" (Galatians 5:22-23). The fruit of the Spirit is the product of HOLY SPIRIT.

The HOLY SPIRIT also works in us through the WORD OF GOD. HE uses the power of Scripture to convince us and influence our way of thinking. HE does this to form us into godly people. As we build a closer relationship with the Holy Spirit, he will also pull us away from things we have in our lives that do not please him. This can be as simple as inappropriate music becoming distasteful to us because of the negative messages it brings, for example. The point is, when the HOLY SPIRIT is at work in our life, it is evident all around us. The Bible says that "All Scripture is inspired by GOD and is useful to teach us what is true and to make us realize what is wrong in our lives. It corrects us when we are wrong and teaches us to do what is right. GOD uses it to prepare and equip HIS people to do every good work." (2nd Timothy 3:16-17). HOLY SPIRIT makes us more like CHRIST.

We already know the goal of the HOLY SPIRIT'S work is to make us more like JESUS, but how does HE do this? It is a process known as sanctification. And no, it is not as complicated as it appears! Sanctification is the process of the HOLY SPIRIT disrobing away our sinful habits and bringing us into holiness. Colossians 2:11 describes that "when you came to CHRIST, you were 'circumcised,' but not by a physical procedure. CHRIST performed a spiritual circumcision the cutting away of your sinful nature." (Colossians 2:11).

The HOLY SPIRIT OF GOD works in us by taking away our sinful physical characteristics and changing them into godly characteristics. HIS work in us makes us increasingly like JESUS. HE gave us. Just as Acts 1:8 mentions, the HOLY SPIRIT empowers Christians to be effective witnesses for JESUS CHRIST. HE gives us the boldness to testify of the LORD JESUS CHRIST in circumstances where we would normally be dreadful or timid. "For GOD has not given us a spirit of fear and timidity, but of power, love, and self-discipline" (2 Timothy 1:7). The power that the HOLY SPIRIT gives us is something that reflects in the natural as well as the supernatural. HE gives us power, love, and self-discipline. Power can be many things backed up by the HOLY SPIRIT, such as boldness to preach the gospel and power to perform healing miracles. Love given by the HOLY SPIRIT is obvious when we have the heart to love others the way JESUS would.

 Live a life filled with love for others following the example of Christ, who loved you and gave himself as a sacrifice to take away your sins. And God was pleased because that sacrifice was like sweet perfume to him (Ephesians 5:2)

The self-discipline that is given by the HOLY SPIRIT allows a person to follow through on GOD'S will and have wisdom throughout life. The self-discipline that is given by the HOLY SPIRIT allows a person to follow through on GOD'S will and have wisdom throughout life. What JESUS is telling us here is that when we have the HOLY SPIRIT in our lives, HE will guide us in the direction we need to go. The HOLY SPIRIT will not leave us in confusion but will reveal the truth to us. HE illuminates the dark areas of our lives to give us an unobstructed vision of GOD'S purpose for us. In the Book of Romans, it says "For all who are led by the SPIRIT OF GOD are children of GOD. So, you have not received a spirit that makes you fearful slaves. Instead, you received GOD'S SPIRIT when HE adopted you as His own children." (Romans 8:14-17).

The Scripture itself is comprehensive and dependable, but impossible to comprehend without the help of the HOLY SPIRIT. The HOLY SPIRIT imparts and reveals the meaning of Scripture to Believers the way JESUS would. The Bible states that "All Scripture is inspired by GOD and is useful to teach us what is true and to make us realize what is wrong in our lives. It corrects us when we are wrong and teaches us to do what is right." (2nd Timothy 3:16). "But the Helper, THE HOLY SPIRIT, whom the FATHER will send in MY NAME, HE will teach you all things and bring to your remembrance all that I said to you" (John 14:26). "When the SPIRIT of truth comes, HE will guide you into all truth. HE will not speak on HIS own but will tell you what HE has heard. HE will tell you about the future." The HOLY SPIRIT guides us into all truth. HE will not speak on HIS own but will tell you what HE has heard. HE will tell you about the future." Pointless to say, the HOLY SPIRIT is our leader and those who follow HIM are HIS children.

Understanding the HOLY SPIRIT: To grip how GOD'S SPIRIT works within us, we must understand what GOD'S SPIRIT IS. Some believers are confused on this point. First, understand that the HOLY SPIRIT is not a separate "person," along with GOD THE FATHER AND JESUS CHRIST, forming a "HOLY TRINITY." This is not biblical evidence to support the common belief that the HOLY SPIRIT is a separate person, but together with the FATHER and the SON. In Scripture, the HOLY SPIRIT instead is described most often as the power of GOD at work in our lives. This power originates from HEAVENLY FATHER, allowing us to be "led by the SPIRIT OF GOD" (Romans 8:14). What does GOD'S HOLY SPIRIT do for us as Christians? This question affects the fundamental of our religious beliefs, because without the power of GOD'S SPIRIT we can have no deep, close relationship with the HEAVENLY FATHER, nor can we become His children. It is because the Spirit dwells in us that we are called the children of GOD (Romans 8:14-17). We must understand what it means to be "led by SPIRIT." GOD'S SPIRIT does not drive, drag, or push us around; it leads us. It will not prevent us from sinning, nor will it force us to do what is right. It leads us, but we must be willing to follow.

> **But in fact, it is best for you that I go away,**
> **because if I do not, the Advocate will not come.**
> **If I do go away, then I will send him to you.**
> **(John 16:7)**

CHAPTER 6

WHO WILL NOT MAKE HEAVEN!

The Scripture already said that many people will not make HEAVEN. Our LORD JESUS CHRIST has been strong and clear about a point that can be difficult to understand: HE has not come to abolish the Law of Moses, but to fulfill it. It will not pass away until all has been accomplished. Those hearing JESUS' message should not be compassionate on themselves or their students about obeying the commands of the law. Those who obey them will be called great in the kingdom of HEAVEN; those who do not carefully obey them will be called the least. This does not suggest that good deeds earn salvation, but it does make an important point about GOD'S intent for those prior messages (Matthew 5:17–19). Now JESUS demands a standard which would have sounded impossible to His listeners exactly how it is meant to be taken. Scribes were professional experts on the Scriptures. The Pharisees were a sect famous for their extremely careful keeping of the law of Moses. They were so careful, in fact, that they added layers of detail, rules, and regulations on top of the law, so they had never come close to breaking it. Pharisees were extraordinarily strict with their students and with the common synagoguegoers about what it took to follow the law to be righteous. **Friends, unrepentant sinners will not make Heaven.**

Who Will Not Make It To Heaven?

JESUS is making two distinct points here. Matthew has already shown that the righteousness of the scribes and Pharisees is false. John the Baptist called them out as a "brood of vipers" in need of a repentance that will actually "bear fruit" instead of just looking good to other people (Matthew 3:7–8). One of those who would not make HEAVEN is a RELIGIOUS sin. Idolaters are people who worship a false god, people who have a false religion. They may be moral, but they worship a false god. Their fate will be the lake of fire (Revelation 21:8). JESUS, too, will clash with the Pharisees over the way they work so hard on outward appearances while sin deteriorations go on in their hearts. As CHRIST JESUS will stress in HIS teaching, GOD cares far more about what is in a person's heart than how other people perceive them. OUR HEALVENLY FATHER Values true cleanliness inspired by true love more than mechanical rule-keeping driven by spiritual of pride. So true "righteousness" is healthier than the awful form marched by religious hypocrites.

Individually, we cannot live a life of moral spotlessness worthy of HEAVEN. This is why Apostle Paul was writing in Romans 3:23, "for all have sinned and fall short of the glory of GOD." He will add, though, in the following verse what JESUS' listeners will come to understand later, that those who come to faith in CHRIST "and are justified by HIS grace as a gift, through the redemption that is in CHRIST JESUS" (Romans 3:24). JESUS is prepping HIS hearers to understand that they need righteousness that only HIM is capable to earn for everyone.

$$\Bigg\{ \text{ For many are called, but few are chosen} \atop \textbf{(Matthew 22:14)} \Bigg\}$$

**For many are called, but few are chosen
(Matthew 22:14)**

One of the sins that will stop people from entering HEAVEN is a VERBAL sin. "Revilers" refers to people who say all kinds of hateful things out of their mouth and are verbally abusive. There are many people who would not think of committing some gross sexual sin but do this all the time. They insult and ridicule people. Are you a reviler? Do you slander people? When THE LORD JESUS CHRIST was reviled and insulted, HE did not revile people back (I Peter 2:23). We are not even supposed to associate with professing Christians who are revilers (I Corinthians 5:11).

Our LORD JESUS CHRIST made open declarations that not everyone who refers to HIM as "LORD" will enter the kingdom of HEAVEN. The title of "LORD" suggests an expert, a leader, and someone to whom the speaker submits. In prior teaching, JESUS indicated that mere words and actions are not enough they must be motivated by sincerity and truth (Matthew 6:1, 5, 16). In that same way, JESUS states directly that merely referring to HIM as LORD is not enough. Neither are acts of righteousness. Entrance to the KINGDOM OF HEAVEN IS limited to those who truly, fully do the will of HIS FATHER IN HEAVEN (2 Corinthians 13:5). That starts with sincere faith in CHRIST (John 6:28–29) and extends to humility in how we live our lives (John 14:15). Not everyone calls out to ME, 'LORD! LORD!' will enter the KINGDOM OF HEAVEN. Only those who do the will of my will enter. (Matthew 7:21).

There is a two-sided warning about false believers in (Matthew 7:15–23). A religious leader may appear respectable and wise, but before making these conclusions, you must look at the fruit of his/her life to know if he/she truly represents GOD. In the same way, it is possible for a person to claim to follow JESUS, referring to HIM as "LORD," when they are not true believers. Only those who do the WILL of the FATHER will be allowed into the KINGDOM of HEAVEN which JESUS defines as beginning with true belief (John 6:28–29). Our good works might fool other people, and might even fool ourselves, but they cannot fool GOD. And HE said: "I tell you the truth, unless you change and become like little children, you will never enter the KINGDOM OF HEAVEN.

THE SWORD OF SPIRIT made it clear to each one of us about which individuals will be seen in HEAVEN. In the Book of Revelation, it speaks about those who will stand before the Great White Throne of Judgment. "And if anyone's name was not found written in the book of life, he was thrown into the lake of fire" (Revelation 20:15). Not everyone will be in HEAVEN, because not everyone puts their faith in GOD for their redemption.

Even before JESUS came, people were redeemed and justified before GOD by faith, "For if Abraham was justified by works, he has something to boast about, but not before GOD. For what does the Scripture say? 'Abraham believed GOD, and it was counted to him as righteousness.' Now to the one who works, his wages are not counted as a gift but as his dues. And to the one who does not work but believes in him who justifies the ungodly, his faith is counted as righteousness" (Romans 4:2-5). JESUS declares that not everyone that says "LORD, LORD" will enter the KINGDOM OF HEAVEN, for there will be some who have labored by prophesy in HIS name, have cast out devils and have done great works, but they will miss HEAVEN. There will be people who stand before CHRIST at judgment that will be incredibly surprised at the fact that they will not enter HEAVEN.

{
For many are called, but few are chosen
(Matthew 22:14)
}

CHAPTER 7

CLINGING TO GOD!

Run to the TRINITY, GOD THE FATHER, GOD THE SON AND GOD THE HOLY SPIRIT! To "cling" to GOD is to trust in HIS promises, to seek HIS favor, to care only for HIS approval and not for that of men, to invest time in HIS service, and to always keep HIS praise on your lips" (Ps. 63:7-8). Do you CLING to JESUS as your SAVIOR and RESCUER? "Have you put your TRUST in JESUS as THE LORD of your life? Do you RELY upon HIM and HIS WORD in your daily life and decisions? If you have, you know it, and truthfully, so does everyone else who knows you. These powerful transformations cannot be hidden. At least a few individuals that have known you for a long time will not be aware of this. By us clinging to GOD, will fuel us to HEAVEN. There is no way that we cling to GOD and not make HEAVEN.

I am convinced that there are: Several Ways to Cling to GOD: One of the ways to cling to GOD is to retain your dedication to HIM: The enticement to forget GOD is continuously present. Nevertheless, there is a way to uphold one's dedication to the LORD. According to the counselling of Joshua; Joshua 23:6-11; ought to help us in keeping our commitment to GOD. 6 "So be incredibly careful to follow everything Moses wrote in the Book of Instruction. Do not deviate from it, turning either to the right or to the left. 7 Make sure you do not associate with the other people remaining on the land. Do not even mention the names of their gods, much less swear by them, serve them, or worship them. 8 Rather, cling tightly to the LORD YOUR GOD as you have done until now. 9 "For the Lord has driven out great and powerful nations for you, and no one has yet been able to defeat you. 10 Each one of you will put to flight a thousand of the enemy, for the Lord your God fights for you, just as HE has promised. 11 So be very careful to love the LORD YOUR GOD.

> **Finally, my brethren, be strong in the Lord and in the power of His might (Ephesians 6:10)**

Satan is the father of all lawlessness; just like he is the father of all liars. The coming of the lawless one is according to the working of Satan, with all power, signs, and lying wonders, ten and with all unrighteous deception among those who perish, because they did not receive the love of the truth, that they might be saved. 11 And for this reason GOD will send them strong delusion, that they should believe the lie, twelve that they all may be condemned who did not believe the truth but had pleasure in unrighteousness (2nd Thessalonians 2:9-12). For the grace of GOD has appeared, bringing salvation for all people, 12 training us to renounce ungodliness and worldly passions, and to live self-controlled, upright, and godly lives in the present age, 13 waiting for our blessed hope, the appearing of the GLORY OF OUR GREAT GOD and SAVIOR JESUS CHRIST, 14 who gave HIMSELF for us to redeem us from all lawlessness and to purify for HIMSELF a people for HIS OWN possession who are zealous for good works. (Titus 2:11-14).

Personally, I began noticing and seeing changes in my life when I asked the LORD to help me to diligently follow HIM IN HIS WORD. I am encouraging all of us to spend quality time in the WORD OF GOD. Pray that GOD would mold you by HIS HOLY SPIRIT; and the LIVING WORD, that HE would provide you with a contrite heart of repentance, that you would walk in a way worthy of the LORD (Romans 12:1-2; Colossians 1:9-10). Do not depend on yourself to clean yourself up. It is going to be impossible for anyone to succeed. You must be completely dependent upon the GRACE OF GOD. Look to JESUS CHRIST and pursue after HIM with everything you have, and forget about what your associates, family, and social spheres think about you and your walk with CHRIST.

The moment you confess CHRIST as your LORD and SAVIOUR, you will be mocked and ridiculed by your old friends and your associates. Brethren, does it really matter? After I became a born-again believer, I distanced myself from most of my friends and family members because I had no desire to do those things I used to do with them any longer. I determined to pursue my SAVIOR JESUS CHRIST. This established in me self-control, discipline, and a hatred for the things that displease GOD and bring reproach to the name of JESUS. GOD created me to bring pleasure to HIS NAME. By the GRACE OF GOD, I have determined to do that for the rest of my life.

Pay attention to GOD'S WORD. GOD ALMIGHTY never blesses disobedience. Always pray for the Spirit of discernment. An awareness filled with WORD OF GOD can analytically assess worldly society and could see through the empty values of the current creation and resist integration. A unique sign of imminent rejection of GOD is a fading respect for the AUTHORITY OF HIS WORD. There is doubt that any contempt for Biblical inspiration is constantly the first step in the direction of spiritual rebellion. Joshua is talking about "keeping" and "doing" GOD'S WORD, not simply giving tacit consensus to its rights. We must be "strong" to keep it and do it and not depart from it also to the right or to the left. Any disrespect for Biblical inspiration is always the first stage toward spiritual rebellion.

Avoid pagan impact. In the book of Joshua 23:6-11, Do we notice the connection between verses 6 and 7. I believe that the only way one avoids life shaped after the image of pagan society is precisely by keeping and doing GOD'S WORD. There will be times and temptation to think that the world has it better than we do.

Pay close attention to all my instructions. "You must not call on the name of any other gods. Do not even speak their names" (Exodus 23:13). But if you have Scripture on your lips and the praise of GOD'S name in your mouth, you will not have room or time for even so much as accepting anything else. We cling to what is decent by clinging to the LORD. JESUS CHRIST in us is completely the goodness we required to be exclusively virtuous.

> **Finally, my brethren, be strong in the Lord and in the power of His might (Ephesians 6:10)**

Completely surrender yourself to GOD (Joshua 23 vs 8) The word "cling" in this verse is translated "hold fast" or "cleave" in Genesis 2:24, where GOD says a man should leave his father and mother and "cleave" to his wife (liken its use in Deut. 10:20-21; 11:22; and 13:4). Visualize the intimate encirclement of spouses, or a young youngster holding fast to his father's hand. To "cling" to GOD is to stay so close to HIM that no sin can get between you and HIM. To "cling" to GOD is to purposefully spend time alone with your HEAVENLY FATHER for prayer and praise and the study of HIS WORD. To "cling" to GOD is to trust in HIS PROMISES, to seek HIS favor, to care only for HIS approval and not for that of men, to invest time in HIS service. Continuously keep HIS praise on your lips (Ps. 63:7-8). To cling to GOD is to become allergic to sin. Avoid anything that will bring displeasure to HIM.

Promote a profound love for GOD in every way (vv. 9-11). "Be very careful to love the LORD your GOD" (Joshua 23 vs 11). The emphasis is on a relationship of intimacy: "I am yours and you are mine!" GOD is not just GOD. HE is "yours" and "my" GOD because of HIS desire to give HIMSELF to us in covenant loyalty. HIS desire for us is unending. Even though the enemies we face today are not those that Joshua and the people of Israel came across, the approach for confronting them remains much the same. You shall fear the LORD Your GOD; you shall serve HIM and cling to HIM, and you shall swear by HIS NAME (Deuteronomy 10:20). You shall follow the LORD your GOD and fear HIM; and you shall keep HIS commandments, listen to HIS voice, serve HIM, and cling to HIM (Deuteronomy 13:4). But you are to CLING TO THE LORD YOUR GOD, as you have done to this day (Joshua 23:8). For he clung to the LORD; he did not depart from following HIM, but kept HIS commandments, which the LORD had commanded Moses (2 Kings 18:6). For if you are careful to keep all this commandment which I am commanding you to do, to love the LORD your GOD, to walk in all HIS ways and hold fast to HIM (Deuteronomy 11:22).

In the Scripture, GOD warned the people of Israel to turn away from their corrupt behavior and "do what is good" (Amos 5:14). If they would go against the prevailing corruption by hating evil behavior and clinging to what is good and righteous, if they would defend justice instead of trampling on it (Amos 5:10–12), the Lord would stand by them as their defender rather than as their judge. Similarly, Apostle Paul declared that to those who "keep on doing good, seeking after the glory and honor and immortality that GOD offers," the LORD will give eternal life. "But HE will pour out HIS anger and wrath on those who live for themselves, who refuse to obey the truth and instead live lives of wickedness" (Romans 2:7–8,). Brothers and sisters, it is left for us to follow the WORD OF GOD to the core if we want to make HEAVEN.

Pray: HOLY FATHER, at present we pray for Christians all over the world whose faith has grown stale. Bring them back to YOU; stir up their love and trust for YOU in their hearts and give them expectation.

Whatsoever has caused them to lose their spirituality, reinstate them to closeness with YOU FATHER in JESUS CHRIST NAME AMEN?

GOD said, "You will seek me and find me when you seek me with all your heart" (Jeremiah 29:13). We seek HIM by getting to know HIM through HIS WORD (John 17:17), accepting HIS SON'S sacrifice for our sin (Romans 10:9), and living a life guided by the power of the HOLY SPIRIT (Galatians 5:16, 25). As we grow in our faith, our knowledge deepens.

(Proverbs 9:10; 2 Peter 3:18). We begin to see life from God's perspective (Isaiah 55:8–9), and, as we obey Him, we acquire wisdom (Psalm 128:1; Proverbs 2:6). So, within that situation, Christians should unconditionally seek spiritual enlightenment. To know GOD and align our will with HIS is the goal of human existence. The more we know JESUS CHRIST, the more enlightened we are (John 1:4–5). Any other path leads only to darkness (Matthew 22:13).

For we are not fighting against flesh-and-blood enemies, but against evil rulers and authorities of the unseen world, against mighty powers in this dark world, and against evil spirits in the heavenly places (Ephesians 6:12 NLT).

CHAPTER 8

WHO IS CARNAL CHRISTIAN?

Many of us who claim to be CHRIST followers leave a careless life that does not represent the life and character of OUR MASTER JESUS CHRIST. CHRIST is LIGHT and so, they that follow HIM must also walk in light. Do people around you witness that love of CHRIST in you? This could be your family members, your colleagues at work, among your associates. Our character as believers could be the only Bible people around us will read and seek to know the LORD JESUS CHRIST that we claim to be in our lives. A CARNAL Christians are those who claim to be JESUS followers yet, they live a life that does not be in alignment with the WORD of GOD. For a Believer to claim that he or she is a Christian and still leave a sinful life. That person is classified as a carnal Christian. My dear friends, the first stage in overcoming anything in this crooked and perverse world is to know JESUS CHRIST. The greatest decision one will ever make in his or her life is becoming a CHRIST follower. Everybody who receives JESUS in their life will need help to grow in their new life journey. Is it possible for a Christian to be a carnal Christian?

To answer this question, it is important to define the word "carnal." The word "carnal" is translated from the Greek word "sarkikos," which precisely means "fleshly." This expressive word is seen in the setting of Christians in 1st Corinthians 3:1-3. The Apostle Paul was addressing the audience as "brethren," a word he uses to refer to other Christians; he then goes on to label them as "carnal." in this passage. Consequently, we can conclude that Christians can be carnal. The Bible made it undeniably clear that no one of us is sinless (1 John 1:8). Every time we sin, we act carnally. Jesus referred to Sodom and Gomorrah, the infamous cities from Genesis 19 that GOD destroyed for their moral depravity. JESUS said that it will be more tolerable (or bearable) for the people of these ancient cities in the day of judgment than for the people who would reject the gospel taught by the apostles.

To live carnally satisfies the flesh rather than pleasing and honoring GOD. A carnal Christian may have accepted the gift of salvation, but not the sanctifying work of the HOLY SPIRIT and transformation of their inner man. Christians who become carnal in their behavior can expect GOD to lovingly discipline them (Hebrews 12:5-11) so they can be restored to close fellowship with HIM and be trained to obey HIM. GOD'S desire in saving us is that we would progressively grow closer to the image of Christ (Romans 12:1-2), becoming increasingly spiritual and decreasingly carnal, a process known as sanctification.

Until we are delivered from our sinful flesh, there will be outbreaks of carnality. For a genuine believer in CHRIST, however, these outbreaks of carnality will be the exception, not the rule.

 Do not copy the behavior and customs of this world, but let God transform you into a new person by changing the way you think. Then you will learn to know God's will for you, which is good and pleasing and perfect (Romans 12:2)

The main thing to comprehend is that while a Christian can be, for a time, carnal, a real Christian will not continue to be carnal for a lifetime. Some of us Christians have ill-treated the awareness of a "carnal Christian" by saying that it is likely for people to come to faith in CHRIST and then continue to live the rest of their lives in a carnal manner, with no indication of being born again or a new creation (2 Corinthians 5:17). Such a concept is unscriptural. James 2 makes it abundantly clear that genuine faith will always result in good work. Ephesians 2:8-10 declares that while we are saved by grace alone through faith alone, that salvation will result in work. Is it possible for a Christian, in a time of disappointment and/or rebellion, appears to be carnal? Of course yes. Will a true Christian remain carnal? Absolutely not!

Believers or Christians who become carnal in their behavior could expect GOD to affectionately discipline them (Hebrews 12:5-11) so they might be restored to close a companionship with HIM and be trained to obey HIM. GOD'S desire in saving us is that we would progressively grow closer to the image of CHRIST (Romans 12:1-2), becoming increasingly spiritual and decreasingly carnal, a process known as sanctification. Until we are delivered from our sinful flesh, there will be outbursts of carnality. For a genuine believer in CHRIST, however, these outbursts of carnality will be the exception, not the rule. All Christians have some area of their lives where they live carnally. We are being perfected, but not yet perfected. Even Paul, a man no one would accuse of being a "carnal Christian," had areas of his life that the Corinthians accused him of living carnally or according to the flesh. Apostle Paul is well-known, that he boasted in response to peer pressure in 2 Corinthians 12:1.

The spirit of a carnal Christian has not been waked and/or does not have the ability to respond to the work and blessings of GOD and may not know GOD in an individual association. Bible knowledge might go to our heads. We could live to the letter of the law like the Pharisees; and not know GOD (Titus 1:16). GOD looks at the heart, searching for HIS love working in and through HIS children (1 Peter 1:1-8). GOD knows that a heart given to HIM holds the power to abandon earthly desires and live the life that GOD has planned. All Christians have some area of their lives where they live carnally. We are being perfected, but not yet perfected. Even Apostle Paul, a man no one would accuse of being a "carnal Christian," had areas of his life that the Corinthians accused him of living carnally or according to the flesh. Paul even noted that he boasted in response to peer heaviness in 2 Corinthians 12:1.

What Does Scripture Teach Us About Carnal Christian?

The word "Christian" is used in numerous different settings these days. Though, only few people comprehend what a "Carnal Christian" is all about. If we search, we will not find the phrase "Carnal Christian" in the Bible, but the Scripture does teach about being carnally minded and living out of our old sin nature or what we inherited as part of humanity. The biblical word translated "carnal" is also translated "flesh" and it denotes mere human nature or the earthly nature of humankind apart from divine influence, and therefore it is prone to sin and opposed to GOD. A Carnal Christian is a believer in CHRIST who is more influenced by their human or earthly nature rather than the nature of GOD. Scripture teaches that we have our treasure in an earthen vessel (2 Corinthians 4:7). An earthen vessel is made from dirt and Genesis 2:7 says that GOD formed Adam from the dust of the ground. We could then say we have what is ours as believers in CHRIST in a body of flesh or dirt. We are also told that when we come to CHRIST, we are a "NEW CREATION" (1 Corinthians 5:17). However, the new creation has to do with our spiritual life and is not a transformation of our old flesh or our carnal body. The issue then is what controls our treasure. Are we as Carnal Christians controlled by our carnal or fleshly sin nature or do, we surrender to the new creation, which is empowered by the SPIRIT OF GOD?

 Do not copy the behavior and customs of this world, but let God transform you into a new person by changing the way you think. Then you will learn to know God's will for you, which is good and pleasing and perfect (Romans 12:2)

"Brothers and sisters, I could not address you as people who live by the SPIRIT but as people who are still worldly mere infants in CHRIST. I gave you milk, not solid food, because you were not yet ready for it. Indeed, you are still not ready. You are still worldly. For since there is jealousy and quarreling among you, are you not worldly? Are you not acting like mere humans? For when one says, 'I follow Paul,' and another, 'I follow Apollos, are you not mere human beings?" 1st Corinthians 3:1-8 "See to it that no one takes you captive through hollow and deceptive philosophy, which depends on human tradition and the elemental spiritual forces of this world rather than on CHRIST." (Colossians 2:8).

A Christian who is living a carnal life is not willing to "present his/her body as a living sacrifice pleasing and acceptable to the FATHER" (Romans 12:2). The degree of submission to GOD'S work in a person's life is indicated by the degree to which they live in the "satisfying the cravings of your sinful nature" (Ephesians 2:3, 1 John 2:16, Galatians 5:19-20, Romans 1:21-28).

The carnal Christian lives in the lust of the flesh, the lust of the eyes, and the boastful pride of life that is from the world (1John 2:15-17). As this world passes away, Bible says some will leave the body of CHRIST so that it might be publicized that not everyone who is a Christian is a Christian (1 John 2:18-19). At this time, the sheep, who know the voice of JESUS (John 10:25-30), will be separated from the goats (Matthew 25:31-46). If the Carnal Christian is truly saved, they are assured that they will not perish (1 Corinthians 3:10-15, John 3:16). A Christian is a person who practices a monotheistic religion based on the life and teaching of JESUS CHRIST. A working definition is someone who has accepted the work of JESUS at the cross and have taken up their cross to follow JESUS CHRIST.

Consequently then, we know that a Carnal Christian is one who is characterized by inner mental attitudes that are not in agreement with GOD'S viewpoint and from our internal perceptual attitudes come our actions. We could then say that a Carnal Christian is one who does not focus upon GOD'S WORD, does not see the necessity of obeying GOD and does not experience the abundant peace and joy that is the believers if they submit to the power of the SPIRIT in their lives rather than being led by their old carnal nature (Galatians 5:16). A Carnal Christian is often very frustrated because the SPIRIT OF GOD is faithful to us and convicts and persuades us that when we are operating out of our carnal flesh, we are not fulfilling GOD'S purpose for us. Our purpose as children of GOD is to bring glory to HIM in all our choices and actions and so since we are not fulfilling our true spiritual purpose, we suffer self-inflicted desolation.

What Is The Remedy For Carnal Christian?

This is a simple question. The Scripture is very clear on this question. The Bible said that we have all sinned and deserve GOD'S judgment. THE HEAVENLY FATHER SENT HIS ONLY SON, to gratify that judgment for those who believe in HIM. JESUS, THE CREATOR AND ETERNAL SON OF GOD, who lived a sinless life, loves us so much that HE died for our sins, taking the chastisement that we deserve, was buried, and rose from the dead according to the Scripture. If we honestly believe and trust this in our heart, receiving JESUS CHRIST alone as our SAVIOR, declaring, "JESUS IS LORD," we will be saved from judgment and spend eternity with GOD in HEAVEN.

{ **Do not copy the behavior and customs of this world, but let God transform you into a new person by changing the way you think. Then you will learn to know God's will for you, which is good, pleasing, and perfect (Romans 12:2)** }

What Is The Answer For Carnal Christian?

How can we be transformed from being a Carnal Christian to being a Spirit-led Christian? This is an interesting question! Apostle Paul in the Book of Romans 12:1-2; he gives us an answer to this question. We find an answer in where we read that you can choose to submit your flesh or carnality as a living sacrifice or what that is set apart unto GOD and not be conformed or formed by the pressure of this world and the flesh. You can be transformed, which is a recurrent process, through allowing the WORD of the SPIRIT to renew your mind so that we may prove or validate, to put to the test, what is good and acceptable or completely pleasant and whole will of GOD. It is GOD'S will then for a Carnal Christian to developed and grow strong in their faith and walk of submission. The ongoing process that takes a believer in CHRIST from a Carnal Christian or what Hebrews calls a "new babe in CHRIST" to one who is involved in growing as a child of GOD is the choice to take in the solid food of the WORD, which equips us as Christians to be able to distinguish or reason what is good and what is evil and what is good and what is better (Hebrews 5:13-14).

Definition of a Carnal Christian:

What Apostle Paul stated about Carnal Christian in the Book of Romans 8:6-7 and in 1st Corinthians 3:1-4. The features articulated of in these passages are that the carnal or bodily mind, which is human perspective, is antagonism against GOD or is anti-GOD. It cannot please GOD, is unable to digest solid divine food, and is filled with strife, envy, and division.

These are very unhealthy spiritual traits, and the reality is that all believers are carnally minded at one time or another. It is a matter of growing up and becoming mature. That is a process that continues daily as we acknowledge our need for grace and submit to the process. We fully surrender to the LORD as He works through every situation in our lives to fit in with HIS IMAGE. So then, we know that a Carnal Christian is one who is characterized by inner mental attitudes that are not in covenant with GOD'S viewpoint and from our inner mental arrogances come our activities.

We may as well then say that a Carnal Christian is one who does not emphasis upon GOD'S WORD, does not see the need of obeying GOD and does not have knowledge of the plentiful peace and joy that is the CHRIST followers if they submit to the power of the Spirit in their lives somewhat than being controlled by their old carnal nature (Galatians 5:16). The SPIRIT OF GOD is faithful to us and convicts and persuades us when we are working out of our carnal flesh, we are not fulfilling GOD'S purpose for us, a Carnal Christian is often very unsatisfied. Our purpose as children of GOD is to bring pleasure to HIM in all that we do in the choices we make and actions; and so, since we are not fulfilling our true spiritual purpose, we suffer self-inflicted sadness.

> **Do not copy the behavior and customs of this world, but let God transform you into a new person by changing the way you think. Then you will learn to know God's will for you, which is good, pleasing, and perfect (Romans 12:2)**

CHAPTER 9

TRUE BELIEVERS WILL MAKE HEAVEN!

Brothers and sisters, if we are truly Christians and maintained the character and lifestyle of CHRIST JESUS; the answer is yes. But if we are deceiving ourselves and living a double standard life we are not going to HEAVEN! HEAVEN IS A PREPARD PLACE FOR PREPARD PEOPLE. GOD IS HOLY so, anyone that claim to be a Christian must be holy. No room for sinners in HEAVEN. We must repent of our sins if we want to spend eternity with CHRIST JESUS. The Scripture explains that everyone on the planet has a problem called sin (Rom. 3:23). Like a disease, it is passed from parent to child; for instance, asthma, cancer, diabetes, etc., and infects most people in that line. The Bible is clear that the cost of our sin is death, meaning if we do not take care of this problem while we are alive, we will have an even bigger problem when we die (Rom. 6:23). However, GOD sent his son JESUS to take care of our problem called sin so that we can be with GOD both now and forever.

This is a gift from GOD to all who will believe in HIM (Rom. 10:9). Everyone who believes has a responsibility to share this good news with those who do not know (Matt. 28:16-20). Everyone who hears this good news has a responsibility to respond. But, what about those who haven't ever heard? "For God so loved the world that He gave His only begotten Son, that whoever believes in Him should not perish but have everlasting life" (John 3:16). The Lord appeared to him and said, "I am GOD Almighty; walk before me faithfully and be blameless. Then I will make my covenant between me and you and will increase your numbers." (Genesis: 17:1-2). GOD'S way to HEAVEN is the only one that counts. And the only one we could trust. Not All Who Claim To Be Christian WILL Go To Heaven!

The Bible says that our sins are what keeps us from ever being with GOD IN HEAVEN: "But your iniquities have separated between you and your GOD, and your sins have hidden HIS face from you, that HE will not hear." (ISAIAH 59:2). "For all have sinned and come short of the glory of God." (ROM. 3:23). The Bible says that the penalty for our sin is Death: "For the wages of sin is Death...." ROM. 6:23 "The soul that sinneth, it shall Die" Ezekiel,18:4; "Without shedding of Blood is no remission of sin" (HEB. 9:22). Death means eternal separation from GOD in a lake of fire. (Rev. 20:11-15). The good news is that our HEAVENLY FATHER is willing to accept JESUS CHRIST'S death as a substitute for ours. "These six things doth the LORD hate: yea, seven are an abomination unto HIM: 17 A proud look, a lying tongue, and hands that shed innocent blood, 18 An heart that deviseth wicked imaginations, feet that be swift in running to mischief, 19 A false witness that speaketh lies, and he that soweth discord among brethren" (Proverbs 6:16-19).

> **For many are called, but few are chosen**
> **(Matthew 22:14)**

This remains to be a tough question and Christians even disagree on the answer. The Bible explains that the nature of our HEAVENLY FATHER is obvious to all even those who have never heard about JESUS (Rom. 1:19-20; Ps. 19:1). But general knowledge about God does not specify whether they will go to heaven. When questions are complicated, the best place to start is with what we do know about GOD. We know that GOD is fair and just, kind and loving. GOD is fair and unbiased. The Bible says that GOD is a just judge who treats people with fairness (Ps. 9:8). GOD treats people the same no matter who they are so no one will ever leave his/her seat feeling as if they were treated unethically. GOD is gracious. The Bible says that GOD is a "compassionate and gracious, slow to anger, abounding in love" (Ps. 103:8-12). He will always act according to his nature. GOD is a loving FATHER. The Bible explains that GOD loves the world (John 3:16-18) because GOD is love. Therefore, any action HE takes will be out of love. The truth that GOD is fair, just, gracious, and loving does not mean people get to do whatever they want and GOD'S ok with it. We parents, when it comes to children, try to be fair, just, and loving and it does not mean children get to play video games and eat candy all day while watching never-ending hours of television. As parents we try to do what is best for our children through rules, limitations, and consequences, even though imposing rules with grace and love.

Hope we are aware that GOD loves the individual who has never heard about JESUS more than we will ever comprehend. We also understand that the nature of GOD is clear to them through creation. They have a responsibility to respond to what they know and understand. GOD'S love will ensure they are treated so that they will one day leave GOD'S presence feeling that they were treated with grace and justice. There are some things we may need to ask GOD to explain when we stand before HIM. We may never be able to fully solve this challenging question here on earth. It is one reason JESUS sent his disciples to share the good news across the globe; HE wanted to make sure everyone knew about GOD'S love. But, what about you? We cannot speak for the person on the other side of the world, but how will you respond to GOD'S good news? What would happen if you embraced the possibility that the GOD of the Bible really did create the world and really does care for you?

In conclusion about the question, if "All Who Claim to Be Christian Go to Heaven"? As human beings, we are all born with a distinctive need to know others and to be known. Having appropriate relationships is vital to having a full and sustaining life, but not everybody has the kind of positive, helpful, and meaningful relationships they need. Numerous people are not even comfortable with the method of meeting new people and making new friends. We believe that life is better lived in a dependable community of people who appreciate the connection to others, we have fashioned a variety of environments that make it easy for us to meet new people and initiate new relationships. First, Hell was created for the devil and demons, not for people. Unfortunately, not all that claim to be Christians do not go to HEAVEN! Therefore, if anyone is in CHRIST, he is a new creation; old things have passed away; behold, all things have become new. Now all things are of GOD, who has reconciled us to HIMSELF through JESUS CHRIST, (2 Corinthians 5:17-18). But if we claim that we are Christians and still lives in sin it becomes obvious that we are deceiving ourselves; and the individual will not go to HEAVEN.

{ **For many are called, but few are chosen
(Matthew 22:14)** }

HEAVEN is a gift to those who believe on JESUS CHRIST. You could never earn it or somehow deserve it. You must receive the gift of eternal life by faith in what JESUS has done. There is no other way. "That if you confess with your mouth the Lord Jesus and believe in your heart that God has raised Him from the dead, you will be saved" (Romans 10:9). We are told in the Bible that "the Lord is patient and long-suffering not willing anyone to perish but all to come to HIM in repentance because judgment day is coming. (2nd Peter 3:8-10). We cannot claim to be Christian and yet not to go to HEAVEN. This means that we are not living in the first place a CHRIST like life. Some says that they Christians and yet does what is not like a Christians. GOD is HOLY all that come to HIM must be HOLY. HEAVEN is a prepared place for prepared people. We are told in the Bible that "He who endures to the end shall be saved" (Matthew 24:13).

Consequently, the yardstick GOD will use to determine who goes to heaven or not will simply be based on whether one believed in the LORD JESUS CHRIST and accepted HIM as their personal LORD and SAVIOR during their time on earth. There are those who call themselves Christians but live lives that are contrary to what they confess to be. They believe that because they have accepted JESUS CHRIST as their SAVIOR, they will get into HEAVEN when they die even if they continue to live like the devil, GOD will welcome them into heaven when they close their eyes in death. Brothers and sisters, it does not go that way.

You must live like a Christian in its entirety. The fact is that people who will go to HEAVEN are those who are TRULY BORN AGAIN WITH THE NEW NATURE OF CHRIST in them and have accepted JESUS CHRIST as their personal LORD AND SAVIOR by trusting in HIM by faith for their salvation.

Brothers and sisters, not all that claim to be Christians will go to HEAVEN. One must faithfully maintain the life of a Christian. You must live a HOLY life. You will know that you are going to HEAVEN even when you close your eyes in death today after leaving this earth if you have obtained forgiveness and pardon for your sins after being saved and remained saved. Another important thing is through the holy life, you are living, and you will know that you are on your way to HEAVEN as Matthews 5:8 say that only those with a holy and pure heart will see GOD in HEAVEN. Additionally, Romans 8:16 tells us that the HOLY SPIRIT of GOD bears witness with our spirit or inner man that we are GOD'S children on your way to heaven if you are truly saved. Letting Jesus Christ into your life after true repentance is what will enable you to live a HOLY LIFE in this present evil world which is necessary for you to be with HIM in HEAVEN; In the book of Hebrews, it "says without holiness, no one will see GOD" (Hebrews 12:14). Do not let anyone deceive you not all that claim to be Christians will go to HEAVEN you have to live the life CHRIST has called you live. And so, this suggests that if you do not have the imputed HOLINESS and RIGHTNESS of CHRIST, forget about spending eternity with HIM in HEAVEN which itself is HOLY just as its inhabitants are. Consequently, to sum this up if you want to go to Heaven, you must be saved and live a HOLY life while here on earth and by HIS grace mentioned in Titus 2:11, you will do it if you are willing to.

"Not everyone who says to me, 'LORD, LORD,' will enter the KINGDOM OF HEAVEN "only the one who does the WILL OF MY FATHER IN HEAVEN. 22 On that day, many will say to me, 'LORD, LORD, didn't we prophesy in your name, and in your name cast out demons and do many powerful deeds?' 23 Then I will declare to them, 'I never knew you. Go away from me, you lawbreakers!'" (Matthew 7:21-23).

{ **For many are called, but few are chosen (Matthew 22:14)** }

CHAPTER 10

LEARN FROM THE 10 VIRGINS

It is important for us to take adequate lesson from the Parable of the Ten Virgins in (Matthew 25:1–13); we must admit straightforward that there has been much argument as to the meaning of these disputes of our SAVIOR. At least one aspect of this fable can be known with a foregone conclusion. The bridegroom is JESUS CHRIST, and this parable describes HIS return. In the Old Testament (Isaiah 54:4–6; 62:4-5; Hosea 2:19), GOD pictures HIMSELF as the "HUSBAND" of Israel, and in the New Testament (John 3:27–30; Matthew 9:15; Mark 2:19–20), CHRIST is pictured as the BRIDEGROOM OF THE CHURCH. The Church is described in Bible as the BRIDE OF CHRIST (Ephesians 5:25–32). The question here is how ready are we? Remember they were all virgins, but not all of them were ready. This means that we need to be ready for the bridegroom when he comes.

I remembered when I was a small girl in grade school my mother would make a list of household tasks I had to do after school. Despite all these house chores, I still must do my schoolwork. When it comes to my schoolwork, my father will make sure that I do not neglect my school assignments. It is my responsibility to make sure that my schoolwork was not neglected because of house chores. This is exactly how I see the story of the ten Virgins in Scripture. The ten virgins were all equally warned not to be careless about entering the bridegroom into the chamber. The ten virgins were groomed to be ready to usher the bridegroom in when he came. Just like most of us Christians conducts our lives with a non-care attitude; this is exactly what happened to the virgins. Know that this is not exactly like our present-day wedding. Let us see they are all virgins preparing to welcome the bridegroom, they were all instructed to be vigilant and extremely ready/careful; but due to the distraction of this world along the way they became careless with getting the amenities which will enable them to enter the chamber while the bridegroom comes. Five of the ten virgins were foolish while the other five were wise. The five foolish virgins had attitudes that I did not care about, while the five wise virgins were careful with the instructions given to them. NEVER RUN OUT GAS BE LIKE THE FIVE WISE VIRGINS WHO DID NOT RUN OUT GAS. LORD, HELP US TO BE READY and VIGILANT ABOUT THE COMING OF THE GROOM.

The story of ten virgins is a scaring story to me as I run my Christian race. This is an indication that no one is above mistake. Every one of us needs to be alert and be careful about the second coming of OUR LORD AND SAVIOR JESUS CHRIST. The story of the ten virgins reminds me of us believers sleeping when we suppose to watch out for the signs of CHRIST return. In the Book of Matthew 13; Here is another story Jesus told:

{
For many are called, but few are chosen.
(Matthew 22:14)
}

"The Kingdom of Heaven is like a farmer who planted good seed in his field. 25 But that night as the workers slept, his enemy came and planted weeds among the wheat, then slipped away. 26 When the crop began to grow and produce grain, the weeds also grew. 27 "The farmer's workers went to him and said, 'Sir, the field where you planted that good seed is full of weeds! Where did they come from?' 28 "'An enemy has done it!' the farmer exclaimed (Matthew 13:24-28).

The historical situation can also be recognized with a fair amount of confidence. In relating to a first-century Jewish wedding, according to D.A. Carson in the Expositor's Bible Commentary, who defines the setting this way: "Generally the husband-to-be with some close friends left his home to go to the bride's home, where there were numerous ceremonies, trailed by a convoy through the streets after nightfall to his home. The ten virgins may be bridesmaids who have been assisting the bride; and they expect to meet the groom as he comes from the bride's house. Every person in the parade was expected to carry his or her own torch. Those without a torch would be expected to be party crashers or even lawbreakers. The celebrations, which might last several days, would officially get under way at the groom's house." The torch was also a lamp with a minor oil container and wick or a rod with a rag soaked in oil on the end of it which would have need of intermittent re-soaking to uphold the flame. Of explanatory meaning is which return of CHRIST is this? Is it HIS return for the rapture of the Church, or is it HIS return to set up the Idealistic Kingdom at the end of the Tribulation? Dispensational scholars are divided over this crucial issue, and for now no effort will be made to answer this question here. Irrespective of which return it is, the lessons to be learned are appropriate to both.

The Ten Virgins: What It Means to Be Ready! (Matthew 25:1-13)

"Then shall the kingdom of heaven be likened unto ten virgins, which took their lamps, and went forth to meet the bridegroom. 2 And five of them were wise, and five were foolish. 3 They were foolish they took their lamps and took no oil with them: 4 But the wise took oil in their vessels with their lamps. 5 While the bridegroom tarried, they all slumbered and slept. 6 And at midnight there was a cry made, Behold, the bridegroom cometh; go ye out to meet him. 7 Then all those virgins arose and trimmed their lamps. 8 And the foolish said unto the wise, give us of your oil; for our lamps are gone out. 9 But the wise answered, saying, "not so; let there be not enough for us and you: but go ye to them that sell, and buy for yourselves. 10 And while they went to buy, the bridegroom came; and they that were ready went in with him to the marriage: and the door was shut. 11 Afterward also came the other virgins, saying, Lord, Lord, open to us. 12 But he answered and said, Verily I say unto you, I know you not. 13 Watch therefore, for ye know neither the day nor the hour wherein the Son of man cometh" (Matthew 25:1-13). The five foolish virgins did not really run out of oil; they never had it. Verse 3 of 25 confirmed that they did not have any oil in the first place.

We would do well to remind ourselves of the context before we get to the parable. In answer to the disciples' demand to know what sign would signal OUR LORD'S coming and the end of the age (Matthew 24:3), JESUS spoke to them about the last days. HE made it clear that the end would not come instantaneously, but only after momentous time and troubles (Matthew 24:4-31). OUR LORD issued various warnings (Matthew 24:4-5, 10-11, 23-28), because during these troubled times there would be many intruders, who would seek to turn men's attention and affections away from JESUS, the TRUE MESSIAH. In verses 32-51 of chapter 24, JESUS speaks of what HIS disciples can and cannot know, and based on both, He gives some specific words of instruction regarding the last times.

{
For many are called, but few are chosen.
(Matthew 22:14)
}

The general and simply seen thrust of the parable is that CHRIST will return at an unidentified hour and that HIS followers (believers) must be ready. Being ready means get ready for whatever eventuality arises in our lives and keeping our eyes always fixed on JESUS while we enthusiastically wait for HIS coming. For instance, seen in the fact that all the virgins were sleeping when the call came shows that it does not matter what we are doing when CHRIST returns. We may be pursuing leisure activities, engrossed in the things of this world, working, eating, or sleeping. Whatever it is, we must be doing it in such a way that we do not have to "make things right" (get more oil) when HE comes. This would apply to either the coming of CHRIST for HIS Church or for the Tribulation saints as they wait for HIS second coming.

Getting ready for our LORD'S return includes one major thing which manifests itself in numerous parts of our lives. If we would be ready for CHRIST'S return, we must be born again through saving faith in JESUS CHRIST HIS death, burial, and accurate resurrection from the dead (John 3:16; 14:6; Romans 10:9 and 10; 1 Corinthians 15:1-4; Ephesians 2:1-10). Saving faith in JESUS CHRIST will manifest itself in every aspect of our lives. The fruit of the Spirit (Galatians 5:22) will begin to show. A desire for greater holiness and less sin will be apparent. And a dependable looking for HIS coming will mark our lives. One of the best passages speaking what redeeming quality and faith look like in a believer's life is Titus 2:11-14, "For the grace of God that brings salvation has appeared to all men. It teaches us to say 'No' to ungodliness and worldly passions, and to live self-controlled, upright and godly lives in this present age, while we wait for the blessed hope the glorious appearing of our great GOD and SAVIOR, JESUS CHRIST, who gave HIMSELF for us to redeem us from all wickedness and to purify for himself a people that are his very own, eager to do what is good."

The five virgins who have the extra oil represent the truly born again who are looking with enthusiasm to the coming of CHRIST.

They have saving faith and have determined that, whatever occurs, be it long time or opposing situations, when JESUS returns, they will be looking with eagerness. The five virgins without the oil signify false believers who enjoy the benefits of the Christian community without true love for CHRIST. They are more worried about the party than about desiring to see the bridegroom. Their expectation is that their association with true believers ("give us some of your oil" of verse 8) will bring them into the kingdom at the end. This, of course, is never the case. Off course, one person's faith in JESUS cannot save another. The "LORD, LORD" and "I do not know you" of verses 11 and 12 fit very well with JESUS' condemnation of the false believers of Matthew 7:21-23, "Not everyone who says to ME, 'LORD, LORD,' will enter the KINGDOM OF HEAVEN, but he who does the WILL of MY FATHER who is in HEAVEN will enter. Many will say to ME on that day, LORD, LORD, did we not prophesy in YOUR NAME, and in YOUR NAME cast out demons, and in YOUR NAME perform many miracles?' And then I will declare to them, 'I never knew you; depart from ME, you who practice lawlessness." May we not be found "going away to make the purchase" (v. 10) when CHRIST returns. Take the time now to fill your lamp with oil and take extra along. Continue waiting and observing with joy and expectation of the return of OUR LORD AND SAVIOR JESUS CHRIST.

{ **For many are called, but few are chosen
(Matthew 22:14)** }

Conclusion Of The Parable Of Ten Virgins

All the ten virgins waited for the groom to arrive. Time went by and darkness set in. The husband to-be stayed longer than anticipated and so all ten maids of honor (virgins) slept until the groom arrived. Unexpectedly, at twelve midnight someone cried that the groom was approaching. All ten virgins are awake by this cry, and they start to prepare their lamps for traditional service. The necessity for these lamps is now particularly obvious (it is midnight, pitch dark). The five foolish virgins asked the five wise virgins to share their oil, but their request was denied. It was not like the five wise virgins did not care; it was because there would not be enough oil for all ten lamps. It is better to have a lamplight parade with five working lamps than with ten non-functioning, lightless, lamps.

The foolish virgins were told to go and purchase their own oil, which they did. But during their nonappearance the torchlight parade took place, and the groom, escorted by the five wise virgins entered the festivity hall. The doors were then closed. The five foolish virgins arrived later with oil, but it was too late for them. That portion of the celebrations had already been completed. There was no need for the services of these five virgins, and they were not permitted to enter and join in the wedding festivity. Even though the five virgins begged, "LORD, LORD." they were sent away with the words, "I DO NOT KNOW YOU!" Our LORD then concludes this parable by applying it to HIS disciples (and thus the church). HE urges HIS disciples to stay alert, because they, too, do not know the day or the hour of HIS return. THIS SHOULD BE A BIG LESSON TO ALL BELIEVERS. LORD, HELP US TO BE READY FOR YOUR RETURN IJMN AMEN.

THE PARABLE OF THE WEEDS (Matthew 13: 24–30, 36–43)

The Parable of the Wheat & Weeds teaches us that GOD does have a plan for this world, and HE is working to accomplish it. Though, it is telling overtime and that means there is some waiting to do, we find it challenging. JESUS is teaching us patience the patience of a GOD who chooses to delay HIS judgment. The weeds represent those people who do not listen to GOD'S WORD, they live "I don't care life" they are "sons of the evil one" who will go to the fiery furnace of hell at judgement day. The harvest workers are the angels and harvest time is the end of the age. This means that in this World, good and wicked people will grow and live together. What is our takeaway with lesson of the parable of the weeds among the wheat? JESUS makes it clear that in this world, the wheat needs to grow alongside the weeds until the return of SON of MAN. At all times remember the mission of the Church is sowing seeds not removing the weeds. Born again Christians have enough challenges on our hands trying to deal with sin in our own lives, our own families, in the society, friends and our own Churches.

{
For many are called, but few are chosen.
(Matthew 22:14)
}

WHAT WILL BE OUR TAKEAWAY FROM THE PARABLE OF THE WHEAT AND WEEDS?

This should be a big lesson for each one of us. My personal take away from this parable is that as a believer we should not sleep a spiritual sleep at any time in our walk with the LORD. The enemy of our soul is always doing everything to prevent us from following the LORD. He can make us to be lazy, doubt, fear, or not believing the WORD of GOD. JESUS compared the KINGDOM of GOD to a person who sows good seed in a field. While he sleeps, an enemy comes and sow's weeds among the wheat. This would have meant that the two grew up together and their roots would have entangled. To me, there is obvious that both Christians and unbelievers have an enemy that is at work in the world (do not sleep but be alert!). Along with the power of the KINGDOM another that we should not fight in contradiction of evil in all its methods in the time being in our own lives, in the body of CHRIST and in our society. This alertness allows us to live lives on spiritual alert while avoiding the excesses of being ignorant of the devil's arrangements or of becoming excessively preoccupied with his action.

To me, this happens when a Christian leaves his or door open for the enemy to creep in. If you give Satan 1 mile he takes ten miles. He is out to destroy, distract, discourage, and deceive us from following our faith in CHRIST JESUS. He roars like a lion but he is not the true lion. We have the LION OF THE TRIBE OF JUDA.

{
**For many are called, but few are chosen
(Matthew 22:14)**
}

CHAPTER 11

DECEIVED BELIEVERS!

Can a Christian Be Deceived and Still Go To Heaven!

According to the WORD OF GOD, it is cleared stated that many believers will be deceived on the last days. Friends, it is happening right now in our own very eyes. New Living Translation (NLT), the Bible verse that states "many will be deceived" in the last days is found in Matthew 24:5 which says, "For many will come in my name, claiming, 'I am the Messiah,' and will deceive many. Even those who claim to be men and women of GOD are parading themselves deceiving others in the things of GOD. There are so many false prophets operating today in our Churches. There are many dangers of this last days. We are in a difficult time brothers and sisters. When Apostle Paul was writing to Timothy, he reminded him that in the last days there would be very challenging times. Revealing to what the LORD JESUS HIMSELF told HIS followers, "Do not let anyone mislead you, 5 for many will come in my name, claiming, 'I am the Messiah.' They will deceive many" (Matthew 24:4-5). So, the question of whether Christians can be deceived and still make Heaven! Yes, if he or she repents.

Anytime someone repents of their sins, GOD will ALWAYS FORGIVE. The answer is Yes if he or she repents. Is it possible that a Christian become a victim of deception? Yes! Deceptive spirit is from Satan. Just as Satan is the father of all liars, he is also the chief deceiver. Who was the first to be deceived in the Bible? Eve was the first human being to be deceived in Scripture by Satan. According to the foundation of creation, the serpent, the father of all liars, the chief of deception came to Eve in the absence of her husband Adam. The serpent was the shrewdest of all the wild animals the Lord God had made. One day he asked the woman, "Did God really say you must not eat the fruit from any of the trees in the garden?" 2 "Of course we may eat fruit from the trees in the garden," the woman replied. 3 "It is only the fruit from the tree in the middle of the garden that we are not allowed to eat. God said, 'You must not eat it or even touch it; if you do, you will die.'"4 "You won't die!" the serpent replied to the woman. 5 "God knows that your eyes will be opened as soon as you eat it, and you will be like God, knowing both good and evil." 6 The woman was convinced. She saw that the tree was beautiful, and its fruit looked delicious, and she wanted the wisdom it would give her. So, she took some of the fruit and ate it. Then she gave some to her husband, who was with her, and he ate it, too (Genesis 3:1-6).

> Jesus told them, "Don't let anyone mislead you, many will come in my name, claiming, 'I am the Messiah.' They will deceive many (Matthew 24:4-5)

It is wrong to conclude or teach that a Believer cannot be deceived. This teaching is heresy. According to the Book of James, "Do not be deceived, my beloved brethren." I say this theme, not this verse, because this is a repeated verse in the Bible. A repeated verse and a major theme. Have you ever noticed that? "Do not be deceived, my beloved brethren." (James 1:16). Here James addresses the brethren. He said, "do not be deceived, my brethren." My brethren. My beloved brethren. Something for the Christian. The warnings are unbelievably valuable; very appropriate; extremely helpful for the Christian in his walk and in his warfare. And so is this theme of deception. "Do not be deceived: God cannot be mocked. A man reaps what he sows. The one who sows to please his sinful nature, from that nature will reap destruction; the one who sows to please the Spirit, from the Spirit will reap eternal life" (Gal 6:7, 9).

The Apostle Paul has said, "The kingdom of GOD is not meat and drink; but righteousness, and peace, and joy in the Holy Ghost." As I study the Bible, I pictured in my mind that Heaven is harmony, a state or condition of peace, joy, good health, happiness etc. Through all the ages past, the question, "what must I do to enter into HEAVEN?" This question was never answered except through the light of divine information. HEAVEN has never been entered except through GOD'S OWN SON. JESUS IS THE ONLY WAY TO GOD. HE is TRUTH and the WAY. Having entered the state of paradise called HEAVEN, one is safe and saved. If one has not yet entered, there is something from which he must be saved. What is it? What is salvation? Personally, salvation is defined therefore: "Sin, sickness, death, grave, works of darkness and Satan's chain is permanently destroyed." It has been said that all that is needed to experience salvation is to get rid of sin.

Let no man deceive you by any means: for that day shall not come, except there come a falling away first, and that man of sin be revealed, the son of perdition; 4 Who opposeth and exalteth himself above all that is called God, or that is worshipped; so that he as God sitteth in the temple of God, shewing himself that he is God. 5 Remember ye not, that, when I was yet with you, I told you these things? 7 For the mystery of iniquity doth already work: only he who now letteth will let, until he be taken out of the way. 9 Even him, who is coming is after the working of Satan with all power and signs and lying wonders, (2nd Thessalonians 2:3, 4,5,7,9). As Paul closes the book of Galatians, he warns the readers that they should not be deceived. He tells them that they will reap what they sow.

On one occasion a rich young Jewish man came to JESUS, and said to him, "Good Master, what shall I do that I may inherit eternal life?" JESUS told him to keep the commandments. The young man replied, "All these have I observed from my youth." We are told that as JESUS looked on the young man, he loved him, and he said unto him, "One thing thou lackest: go thy way, sell whatsoever thou hast, and give to the poor, and thou shalt have treasure in heaven: and come, take up the cross, and follow me." When the young man heard this requirement, he went away sorrowful, for he had great possessions.

One of the foundational principles of Christianity is the belief that JESUS CHRIST, the SON of GOD, died and was resurrected into eternal life. The Bible promises that those who believe in GOD will also experience a life after death. Eternal life is clearly present in the scriptures, though the specifics remain a mystery to those of us still living. We see this in (1ˢThessalonians 4:14), with the declaration that those who die knowing CHRIST will also be raised with Him after their death. The Apostle Paul describes our "earthly bodies being shed upon death, and new, immortal and imperishable bodies being given to us" (1ˢᵗ Corinthians 15:51-55). This begs the question of where these new "spiritual" bodies are going for the rest of eternity.

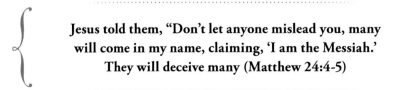

Jesus told them, "Don't let anyone mislead you, many
will come in my name, claiming, 'I am the Messiah.'
They will deceive many (Matthew 24:4-5)

This same Paul discusses his desire to live on earth and his simultaneous desire to die, or depart the earth, to "be with CHRIST" in Philippians 1:23. From this, we can glean that life after death means spending eternity with CHRIST, which is the Biblical concept of HEAVEN. Scriptures assure Christians over and over that they will "be with the Lord forever" (1st Thessalonians 4:17). In John 14:2-3, JESUS says, "I will come back and take you to be with me that you also may be where I am." In Luke 23:43, as He was hanging on the cross moments before His own death, Jesus turned to one of the thieves being crucified next to HIM and said, "today you will be with me in paradise."

This paradise that Christians are promised as their souls' eternal resting place is full of mystery. We cannot say where it is or what dimension, what it looks like, who is there, or what we do there once we have arrived. What the Bible tells us is that if we believe in JESUS CHRIST AS THE SON of GOD, we will be with HIM in HEAVEN after our life here on earth. For many, this idea brings with it great solace. They cannot be certain of where they go but knowing that they will be reunited with GOD is enough. This is often where sacraments like the last rites come into play, or where many people have professed their belief in GOD before dying. We ran to the end. "But he who endures to the end shall be saved" (Matthew 24:13).

Do you CLING to JESUS as YOUR SAVIOR AND RESCUER? "Have you put your TRUST in JESUS as THE LORD of your life? Do you RELY upon HIM and HIS WORD in your daily life and decisions? If you have, you know it, and truthfully, so does everyone else who knows you. These powerful things cannot be hidden, at least not for long. GOD'S HOLY SPIRIT will give you the confidence within yourself to KNOW that you are going to Heaven when you die. He will fill you with His joy, peace, and love and especially the hope of eternal life in HEAVEN. After the video, you can go on to the Roadmap to Heaven which will get you started on your journey to a wonderful new life in CHRIST.

And behold, a man came up to him, saying, 16, "Teacher, what good deed must I do to have eternal life?" 17 And he said to him, "Why do you ask me about what is good? There is only one who is good. If you would enter life, keep the commandments." 18 He said to him, "Which ones?" And Jesus said, "You shall not murder, You shall not commit adultery, You shall not steal, You shall not bear false witness, 19 Honor your father and mother, and You shall love your neighbor as yourself." 20 The young man said to him, "All these I have kept. What do I still lack?" 21 Jesus said to him, "If you would be perfect, go, sell what you possess and give to the poor, and you will have treasure in heaven; and come, follow me." 22 When the young man heard this he went away sorrowful, for he had great possessions". 23 And Jesus said to his disciples, "Truly, I say to you, only with difficulty will a rich person enter the kingdom of heaven. 24 Again I tell you, it is easier for a camel to go through the eye of a needle than for a rich person to enter the kingdom of God." 25 When the disciples heard this, they were greatly astonished, saying, "Who then can be saved?" 26 But Jesus looked at them and said, "With man this is impossible, but with God all things are possible" (Matthew 19:16-26).

Be not deceived; God is not mocked:
for whatsoever a man soweth, that
shall he also reap (Galatians 6:7)

The Book of Revelation describes HEAVEN as a beautiful place with streets made of gold, no suffering, gates of pearl, no sorrow, and infinite beauty; all these wonderful attribute's pale in comparison to the joy that being in the eternal presence of GOD will bring forever. However, human beings who live their life in rebellion against GOD, cannot be in the LORD'S HOLY PRESENCE in sin, and therefore cannot go to HEAVEN on his/her own merits. To remedy the issue of man's sinful nature, GOD sent HIS SON JESUS to die and bear the punishment for the sins of the entire world, and JESUS was resurrected three days later. If someone acknowledges their sin, repents of it, and accepts JESUS as THE LORD of their life, and HIS substitution for us on the cross, placing their faith in HIM, that person can spend eternity with their SAVIOR in HEAVEN. The bottom line is that if you do not accept what JESUS did for you on the Cross over two thousand years ago, YOU WILL NOT ENTER HEAVEN WHEN YOU DIE. It is only two ways HEAVEN OR Hell! We have an opportunity to choose now. Tomorrow might be too late. Today is the day of Salvation. Choose CHRIST and live.

We are told in one of JESUS' parables that Lazarus the beggar died and was carried by the angels into Abraham's bosom. A rich man also died, and in hell (a state of material awareness) he lifted his eyes and saw Abraham and Lazarus afar off. Then he pleaded, "Father Abraham, have mercy on me, and send Lazarus, that he may dip the tip of his finger in water, and cool my tongue; for I am tormented in this flame. But Abraham said, Son, remember that

thou in thy lifetime receivedst thy good things, and likewise Lazarus evil things: but now he is comforted, and thou art tormented." Lazarus may not have overcome all material thoughts, yet he was comforted; hence his thoughts and desires must have been less material than those of the rich man, for he was happier than he, and the rich man still believed in pain in matter and wanted to experience relief by having past poor Lazarus apply water to his tongue.

While JESUS was on the mount of transfiguration, with Peter, James, and John, through his exalted understanding he put aside the belief that separates the so-called here and the hereafter. JESUS showed HIS disciples that there is no difference between these except as thought, probation, and progress make the modification. Through HIS greater spiritual illumination, JESUS transcended the mortal belief of existence for Peter, James, and John, and proved to them that Moses and Elias, who, as the Scriptures say, "appeared in glory," were still living, and reflecting the light of Life on a higher plane of advancement. Does this age believe that "the KINGDOM of HEAVEN is at hand"? CHRIST JESUS made this announcement two thousand years ago, and ought we not to be far in advance of that age? Have we not the experiences and teachings of the EXPERT to build upon? Have these experiences not been formed into methodical rules by her who has been called to go forward in the battle against sin and sickness and the troubles of life?

The voice cried in the wilderness, "Repent ye: for the KINGDOM of HEAVEN is at hand." That KINGDOM is now here. The prophets and religious leaders of old performed many wonderful miracles, although their age had not been hallowed by the presence of JESUS. Should we not do more wonderful things than those prophets and leaders? Is it not a fact that the coming of CHRIST JESUS, so long foreshadowed, is now upon us, and that CHRIST, Truth, does daily move in our midst and do HIS wonderful healing? Truthfully, the SON OF GOD comes, and if we have the key to the kingdom as HE said, it is ours to stand daily at the gates, and watch. It is ours to learn that for us to reach HEAVEN and to enter upon its pleasure requires constant examination of self, constant growth in love, the unquestionable cleansing from all sin, the overcoming of all belief in the reality of life and substance in matter.

> Jesus told them, "Don't let anyone mislead you, many will come in my name, claiming, 'I am the Messiah.' They will deceive many (Matthew 24:4-5)

CHAPTER 12

HEAVEN IS FOR HOLY PEOPLE!

Who Is Considered To Be Holy?

CHRIST followers are to be imitators of our FATHER GOD. JESUS saved us from the world of sin and from death. We were justified by JESUS death. We are not saved to continue in sin we are saved FROM sin, we cannot continue in sin no more. JESUS CHRIST loved us and gave HIMSELF for us an offering and a sacrifice to GOD for a sweet-smelling aroma. Brothers and sisters, we belong to JESUS CHRIST, and we owe it to HIM and ourselves to follow HIM and stay true to HIM. Those who have clean hands and a pure heart will see GOD, they will know HIM here on earth and go to HEAVEN when they die but those who are unrighteous and who practice the works of the flesh and the works of darkness will not see GOD.

The unrighteous and the sinner the children of disobedience will NOT inherit the KINGDOM of GOD. We were once in darkness, but now we are in the light of the LORD. Now we must walk as children of light and we must expose the works of darkness to what they are. JESUS CHRIST was born as a poor man, died as a criminal, rose up from the grave as the King of all Kings and the LORD of all lords, the firstborn of the dead. The MESSIAH is coming back from HEAVEN to be the KING OF ALL KINGS. HE is coming back to reign and rule the entire world. HE will judge everyone according to his or her work on earth. "WITHOUT HOLINESS NO MAN CAN SEE GOD." Siblings, do all that is within your power to do the right thing while we still have the opportunity. Night is coming when no one can work anymore.

It is important for us to first comprehend what it means to live a holy life to be able to address the question of how to live a holy life or what holiness means. To be holy means to be set apart or separate from sin and evil. GOD is HOLY and we need to be holy also and we need to completely detach ourselves from everything that is evil (1 John 1:5). GOD calls us to be holy, just as HE is (1 Peter 1:16, quoting Leviticus 19:2), but it is vital to understand that apart from GOD this becomes difficult. We must have the HOLY SPIRIT indwelling us and filling us with HIS HOLINESS. We can only live a holy life through the power of the SPIRIT; thus, the first step to living a holy life is to accept JESUS as SAVIOR (Ephesians 1:13). Once we have taken that step of salvation, we are declared righteous (Romans 5:1). But what does it look like to be righteous to live a holy life? In 1 Thessalonians 4:3–8, Paul emphasizes sexual purity as part of holy living: "It is GOD'S will that you should be sanctified: that you should avoid sexual immorality; that each of you should learn to control your own body in a way that is holy and honorable, not in passionate lust like the pagans, who do not know GOD" (verses 3–5).

> **But as he which hath called you is holy, so be
> ye holy in all manner of conversation.
> Because it is written, Be ye holy; for I am holy
> (1 Peter 1:15-17)**

Beyond avoiding sexual immorality and keeping sex within GOD'S design for marriage, we can live a holy life by being obedient to God in all areas of life (1 Peter 1:14–16). Knowing and obeying God's Word is key (John 17:17). Hiding God's Word in our hearts keeps us from sin (Psalm 119:11). When we live in obedience to GOD, we are staying separate from evil. We are offering our bodies as "living sacrifices" to GOD (Romans 12:1–2). The purpose of living a holy life is to glorify GOD and display His nature to those around us (Matthew 5:16). Living a holy life of obedience to GOD is living in true freedom from the bondage of sin (Romans 6:6). It is not always easy to choose obedience to God, especially if we are trying to do it all on our own. Satan would love nothing more than to bring us back into bondage through disobedience. But we have the promise, "You, dear children, are from GOD and have overcome them, because the one who is in you is greater than the one who is in the world" (1 John 4:4). The HOLY SPIRIT will produce Christlikeness in us, and, as we yield to HIM, we can live a holy life (Galatians 5:16).

We should always have this mindset: "Count yourselves dead to sin but alive to GOD in CHRIST JESUS" (Romans 6:11). Whenever we face temptation, we should say, this is not me anymore "I am dead to that! That was part of my old life! I am a new creation in CHRIST!" (2 Corinthians 5:17). To live a holy life, is to separate ourselves from sin, we must see ourselves as GOD does as born-again children of the HIGHEST GOD, clothed with the righteousness of CHRIST. We also have the benefit of being part of the BODY of CHRIST. Fellowship with other Christians and making ourselves accountable to them is a reliable source of strength in living a holy life. As believers, we are called to encourage one another in this matter (Hebrews 10:24–25). Siblings remember, we are not trying to live a holy life to receive salvation; living a holy life is a normal result of being saved by GOD'S grace and filled with HIS SPIRIT. It is also significant to not surrender when we mess up. When we fail, our response should be to confess the sin and keep moving forward in our Christian walk (1 John 1:9). Romans 8:1 says, "There is now no condemnation for those who are in CHRIST JESUS." GOD'S grace does not go away when we make mistakes.

Be Ye Holy As I Am Holy! What Does This Mean?

I believe that when GOD say we should be holy as HE is HOLY; means we are called to be like GOD HIMSELF. We are mandated to separate ourselves from the love of this world. We need to pursue holiness with all our hearts. We need to run after GOD; and cling to HIM all the days of our live. Destroy and put to death the deeds of the flesh and put on the robe of righteousness. GOD is holy and righteous. There is none like HIM, no one as holy as HIM, none as glorious. GOD hates sin and loves righteousness. As it says in Psalm 1:5; regarding the wicked, "Therefore the wicked will not stand in the judgment, nor sinners in the congregation of the righteous" In other words, when the LORD comes to judge the earth, the wicked will not stand. They will be cast out. Because they are not holy, they will not be able to stand before the Lord. Philippians 4:8 puts it this way: Finally, brothers, whatever is true, whatever is honorable, whatever is just, whatever is pure, whatever is lovely, whatever is commendable, if there is any excellence, if there is anything worthy of praise, think about these things.

There is nothing more honorable, just, pure, lovely, commendable, excellent, or worthy of praise than the holiness of God. And the more we "think about these things" the more we savor the holiness of God, the more we will desire to be holy. How do we, "Be holy as I am holy,"? By regularly meditating on, delighting in, and thinking deeply about the glorious holiness of GOD. "You who love the LORD, hate evil! He protects the lives of his godly people and rescues them from the power of the wicked" (Psalm 97:10). In 1 Peter 1:16, it says, "You shall be holy, for I am holy." (1 Peter 1:16). This command from GOD to be holy as I AM HOLY is not an easy task. What Does Be HOLY AS I AM HOLY MEAN? It means we are called to be like GOD himself. We are required to pursue holiness with all our hearts.

> But as he which hath called you is holy, so be ye
> holy in all manner of conversation; Because it is
> written, Be ye holy; for I am holy (1 Peter 1:15-17)

Now the works of the flesh are evident: sexual immorality, impurity, sensuality, idolatry, sorcery, enmity, strife, jealousy, fits of anger, rivalries, dissensions, divisions, envy, drunkenness, orgies, and things like these. I warn you, as I warned you before, that those who do such things will not inherit the kingdom of God (Galatians 5:19-21). But as for the cowardly, the faithless, the detestable, as for murderers, the sexually immoral, sorcerers, idolaters, and all liars, their portion will be in the lake that burns with fire and sulfur, which is the second death" (Revelation 21:8). Or do you not know that the unrighteous will not inherit the kingdom of God? Do not be deceived: neither the sexually immoral, nor idolaters, nor adulterers, nor men who practice homosexuality, nor thieves, nor the greedy, nor drunkards, nor revilers, nor swindlers will inherit the kingdom of God (1Corinthians 6:9-10). "When the Son of Man comes in his glory, and all the angels with him, then he will sit on his glorious throne. Before him, all the nations will be gathered, and he will separate people from one another as a shepherd separates the sheep from the goats. And he will place the sheep on his right, but the goats on the left. Then the King will say to those on his right, 'Come, you who are blessed by my Father, inherit the kingdom prepared for you from the foundation of the world." For I was hungry, and you gave me food, I was thirsty, and you gave me drink, I was a stranger and you welcomed me, (Matthew 25:31-46 ESV).

On the other hand, we need to understand that in the last days there will be a time of trouble. For people will be lovers of self, lovers of money, proud, arrogant, abusive, disobedient to their parents, ungrateful, unholy, heartless, unappeasable, slanderous, without self-control, brutal, not loving good, treacherous, reckless, swollen with conceit, lovers of pleasure rather than lovers of God, having the appearance of godliness, but denying its power. Avoid such people. (2 Timothy 3:1-5 ESV). Just as Sodom and Gomorrah and the surrounding cities, which likewise indulged in sexual immorality and pursued unnatural desire, serve as an example by undergoing a punishment of eternal fire (Jude 1:7 ESV). The first mention of not inheriting the kingdom of GOD is found in Paul's first letter to the church at Corinth. "Do you not know that the wicked will not inherit the kingdom of God? Do not be deceived: Neither the sexually immoral nor idolaters nor adulterers nor male prostitutes nor gay offenders; nor thieves nor the greedy nor drunkards nor slanderers nor swindlers will inherit the kingdom of God "(1 Corinthians 6:9-11).

By saying the wicked will not inherit the kingdom of God, Paul is stating that the wicked are not children of God, nor are they heirs of eternal life (Romans 8:17). I believe that this does not mean that anyone of us who has ever committed one of these sins will be denied entrance to HEAVEN. What distinguishes a Christian's life from that of a non-Christian is the struggle in contrast to sin in addition to the ability to overcome it. A true Believer will always repent, will eventually return to GOD, and will always resume the struggle against sin. Nonetheless the Bible gives no backing for the idea that a person who continually and unrepentantly engages in sin can indeed be a Christian. The 1 Corinthians passage lists sins that, if indulged continuously, identify a person as not being redeemed by CHRIST.

The Christian's response to sin is to hate it, repent of it, and forsake it. We still struggle with sin, but with the power of the HOLY SPIRIT, who is our director who lives in us, we can resist and overcome sin. All believers need to be allergic to sin period. The hallmark of a true Christian is the decreasing presence of sin in his/her life. As Christians grow and mature in the faith, sin has less and less of a grip on us. Of course, sinless perfection is impossible in this life, but our hatred for sin becomes greater as we mature. Like Paul, we are distressed that sin still exists in our flesh, causing us at times to do what we do not want to do and looking to CHRIST for relief from this "body of death" (Romans 7:18-25). If an individual vigorously, continually, and unapologetically lives a homosexual lifestyle, the lifestyle of a thief, a greedy lifestyle, a drunken lifestyle, etc., that individual is showing himself/herself to be unsaved, and such a person will certainly not inherit the KINGDOM OF GOD.

 But as he which hath called you is holy, so be ye holy in all manner of conversation; Because it is written, Be ye holy; for I am holy (1 Peter 1:15-17)

Therefore, be imitators of God as dear children. 2 And walk in love, as CHRIST also has loved us and given HIMSELF for us, an offering, and a sacrifice to GOD for a sweet-smelling aroma. 3 But fornication and all uncleanness or covetousness, let it not even be named among you, as is fitting for saints; four neither filthiness, nor foolish talking, nor coarse jesting, which are not fitting, but rather giving of thanks. 5 For this you know that no fornicator, unclean person, nor covetous man, who is an idolater, has any inheritance in the kingdom of CHRIST and GOD. 6 Let no one deceive you with empty words, for because of these things the wrath of GOD comes upon the sons of disobedience.

7 Therefore do not be partakers with them. 8 For you were once darkness, but now you are light in the LORD. Walk as children of light 9 (for the fruit of the SPIRIT is in all goodness, righteousness, and truth), then find out what is acceptable to the Lord. 11 And have no fellowship with the unfruitful works of darkness, but rather expose them (Ephesians 5:1-11 NKJV).

Do you not know that the unrighteous will not inherit the Kingdom of God? Do not be deceived. Neither fornicators, nor idolaters, nor adulterers, nor homosexuals, nor sodomites, ten nor thieves, nor covetous, nor drunkards, nor revilers, nor extortioners will inherit the Kingdom of God. 11 And such were some of you. But you were washed, but you were sanctified, but you were justified in the name of the Lord Jesus and by the Spirit of our God (1st Corinthians 6:9-11; NKJV). We the believers are to be imitators of our FATHER GOD. JESUS saved us from the world from sin and from death. HE justified us. We are not saved to continue in sin we are saved from sin, to sin no more. JESUS CHRIST loved us and gave HIMSELF for us an offering and a sacrifice to GOD for a sweet-smelling aroma. We belong to HIM, and we owe it to HIM and ourselves to follow HIM and stay true to HIM. Now we must walk as children of light and we must expose the works of darkness to what they are.

Brothers and sisters, those who have clean hands and a pure heart will see GOD; they will know HIM here on earth and go to HEAVEN to be with HIM when they die. But those who are unrighteous and who practice the works of the flesh and the works of darkness will not see our HEAVENLY FATHER. The unrighteous and sinners that is the children of disobedience will NOT inherit the KINGDOM of GOD. We were once in darkness, but now we are in CHRIST JESUS who is the light of GOD. GOD loves everybody but HE hates sin. Sin stinks before GOD. We should run away from sin. No unrighteous person will see GOD.

But as he which hath called you is holy, so be ye holy in all manner of conversation; Because it is written, Be ye holy; for I am holy (1 Peter 1:15-17)

These classes of people will not inherit the KINGDOM OF GOD: Whoremongers or Fornicators (the immoral); male prostitutes; libertines' persons who are morally or sexually unrestrained. He who overcomes shall inherit all things, and I will be his God and he shall be My son. 8 But the cowardly, unbelieving, abominable, murderers, sexually immoral, sorcerers, idolaters, and all liars shall have their part in the lake which burns with fire and brimstone, which is the second death." (Revelation 21:7-8 NKJV). Blessed is those who do HIS commandments, that they may have the right to the tree of life and may enter through the gates into the city. 15 But outside are dogs and sorcerers and sexually immoral and murderers and idolaters, and whoever loves and practices a lie. (Revelation 22:14-15 NKJV). Unclean persons; homosexual; pervert; impure; foul; unclean; immoral; lewd; or demonic.

Effeminate (catamites) of uncertain affinity; soft to the touch; effeminate; figuratively, a catamite. A catamite is a young man who submits his body to unnatural lewdness; a boy or youth who is in a sexual relationship with a man. "Soft to the touch" refers to men who have feminine traits to an inappropriate degree; lacking in manly strength or aggressiveness; especially marked with weakness, softness, and love of ease; excessively affected in his emotions. Abusers of themselves with humanity sodomites; homosexuals; pederasts (lover of boys); lesbians; one guilty of unnatural offenses; sexual pervert; Adulterers (the unfaithful) a (male) paramour; illicit lover; figuratively, apostate (a person who forsakes his religion or his cause); Covetous men; holding or desiring more; eager for gain; avaricious, hence a defrauder. Thieves (robbers); Idolaters (false worshippers); servant or worshipper (literally or figuratively) of an image or an idol; Drunkards (drinkers of intoxicants); a person who is habitually or frequently drunk; Revilers (abusers of others); mischief; abusive, railer: reviler; verbally abusive; to assail with contemptuous or opprobrious (outrageously disgraceful or shameful) language; address or speak of abusively.

Extortionist (those who obtain things by violence or threats); greedy; extortion: ravening; deceivers to cheat; delude; deceive. But evil men and impostors will grow worse and worse, deceiving and being deceived (2 Timothy 3:13 NKJV). "For we ourselves were also once foolish, disobedient, deceived, serving various lusts and pleasures, living in malice and envy, hateful and hating one another" (Titus 3:3 NKJV). And children (sons) of disobedience disbelief; obstinate and rebellious; disobedience; unbelief. 5 "Therefore, put to death your members which are on the earth: fornication, uncleanness, passion, evil desire, and covetousness, which is idolatry.

6 Because of these things the wrath of God is coming upon the sons of disobedience" (Colossians 3:5-6 NKJV). My brothers and sisters let us try to be holy as our HEAVENLY FATHER IS HOLY. BY THE GRACE OF GOD, HE WILL GRANT US THE ABILITY TO BE HOLY AS HE IS HOLY. WE DO NOT HAVE THE STRENTH TO BE HOLY; BUT WITH HIM ALL THINGS ARE POSSIBLE. REMAINED BLESSED.

But as he which hath called you is holy, so be ye holy in all manner of conversation.

Because it is written, Be ye holy; for I am holy
(1 Peter 1:15-17)

CHAPTER 13

GOD MADE A WAY OF ESCAPE!

Why Did GOD Decide To Send HIS SON?

Our CREATOR is GOD ALMIGHTY. There is no other GOD. HE is INVISIBLE GOD, ALPHA AND OMEGA, THE BRIGHT AND MORNING STAR, ANCIENT OF THE DAY, THE LILLY OF THE VALLEY, THE HOLY GOD, THE GLORY OF ISRAEL, A SOVERIEGN GOD THE FIRST AND THE LAST, etc., Since GOD is HOLY, and those who serve HIM must be holy. According to the WORD OF GOD, they that come to HIM must be Holy. If HE is in the light, HIS people must also walk in the light if they truly know HIM. This is an indispensable characteristic of Believers' lives: a firm moral code. Though, such a life is not unbending and legalistic, nor is it an insincere conformity to guidelines and values. It is an ethical code followed out of profound love and devotion, much the same as the fidelity of a loving spouse. We need only contemplate the purposes of GOD in salvation. GOD is concerned not only to save from the punishment of sin, but also to re-create an individual in holiness from the inside out.

Why Did GOD Send HIS SON?

By sending HIS SON JESUS to die for our sins, GOD is working to bring back the happiness of HIS OWN GLORY exceptional in and through us. The apostle John caught this truth very well when he composes: "See what kind of love the Father has given to us that we should be called children of GOD; and so, we are" (1 John 3:1 ESV). SON of GOD is so important in all believers' life; Why did the LORD JESUS need to come from HEAVEN to earth and to be born in Bethlehem's manger? There was a three-fold determination, and this is mentioned in (Galatians 4:5, 6 and 7). Through HIS death and resurrection, JESUS atoned for the sins of humanity, allowing them to be reconciled with GOD. Christianity teaches that CHRIST is the only way to salvation, and that salvation will be for those who believe, as well as those who do not believe. According to the New Testament, JESUS, GOD'S SON, came to earth to reunite us with GOD through the final sacrifice: HIS OWN LIFE. We will never have a life worthy of GOD on our own. Consequently, JESUS lived a life short of sin on our behalf. And then HE died the painful death our sins; yours and mine deserve. I am using this book to encouraging challenging all of us to pursue closeness with GOD every day of our life.

> Since we know that Christ is righteous,
> we also know that all who do what is right
> are God's children (1 John 2:29 NLT)

Why Did JESUS Come?

GOD has opened another way to have reconciled us to HIM. JESUS CHRIST is the way for us to be forgiven of all our sins and robed in perfect righteousness. JESUS CHRIST was without sin, nonetheless, on the cross all our sins were TAKEN OVER BY HIM, and HE died in our place. Here and now by faith in HIM we can be forgiven and cleansed of our sins and made ready for HEAVEN. Do not trust in your own goodness any longer, but by faith put your trust in JESUS CHRIST alone for your salvation and deliverance. HE IS THE ONLY WAY TO GOD.

CHRIST came in order that we might be REDEEMED. To redeem, in this case, means to deliver from the bondage and the curse of the Law. The curse of the Law is the penalty which comes because we have broken the Law, and we all have broken the Law, and therefore we are under the curse and are in danger of punishment. But CHRIST came to redeem us from the curse of the Law, and HE did this by offering HIS life and shedding HIS blood on Calvary's cross look up (1 Peter 1:18-19). Thank GOD, every believer can sing: "Free from the Law, O happy condition, JESUS had bled, and there is remission." He came that we might receive the FULL RIGHTS of sons (verse 5). GOD'S purpose in the manifestation is that we might become sons of GOD, and this son ship is based upon redemption "to redeem that we might receive." The Son of GOD became the SON of man that we, sons of men, might become SONS of GOD. Who, then, are the sons of GOD? They are those who have the Spirit of adoption in their hearts compared to those that don't have the right Spirit.

JESUS came that we might become heirs of GOD through CHRIST (verse 7). Compare Romans 8:16-17, where we are told that we are co-heirs with CHRIST. Because HE shared our humanity, with all the resulting sufferings that are involved, we, by HIS grace and through faith in HIM, are to share HIS glory. In the parable of Luke 15, the father said to his elder son, "My son, you are always with me, and everything I have is yours" (Luke 15:31). This is exactly what our FATHER says to every one of HIS children. But when the time arrived that was set by GOD the FATHER, GOD sent his SON, born among us of a woman, born under the conditions of the law so that he might redeem those of us who have been kidnapped by the law. Thus, we have been set free to experience our rightful heritage. You can tell for sure that you are now fully adopted as his own children because GOD sent the Spirit of his Son into our lives crying out, "ABBAH FATHER!" Doesn't that source of pride of intimate discussion with GOD make it simple that you are not a slave, but a child? And if you are a child, you are also an heir, with whole admittance to the birthright. Jesus told him, "I am the way, the truth, and the life. No one can come to the Father except through me (John 14:6).

GOD Made A Way:

When I was studying one of the Old Testament Book, GOD instructed Moses step by step how the Levites to perform a sacrifice to HIM. Procedures for the Burnt Offering; Procedures for the Grain Offering, Procedures for the Peace Offering and Procedures for Sin Offering etc. Believers will appreciate what GOD did for us by sending JESUS as our HIGH PRIEST. CHRIST is the only one that can keep all these instructions. To be clear on what I am saying, please the Book of Leviticus chapter 1 to 27 to be able to understand what GOD did for us. I was really thanking GOD for JESUS CHRIST, the Sacrificial LAMP, our HIGH PRIEST. The most scaring thing was when fire came from HEAVEN and burned the two sons of Aaron. Moses received instructions from the LORD on how Aaron and his two sons will follow GOD'S instructions to the core. Is either obeying GOD or face the consequences of disobeying HIM. Let us look at what Aaron's sons Nadab and Abihu did that brought GOD'S judgement to both. If ever I appreciated what GOD did for us through JESUS coming from HEAVEN to redeem us, it is after I read the Book of Leviticus.

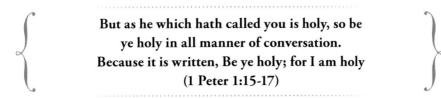

**But as he which hath called you is holy, so be
ye holy in all manner of conversation.
Because it is written, Be ye holy; for I am holy
(1 Peter 1:15-17)**

The Sin of Nadab and Abihu: "Aaron's sons Nadab and Abihu put coals of fire in their incense burners and sprinkled incense over them. In this way, they disobeyed the Lord by burning before him the wrong kind of fire, different than what he had commanded. So fire blazed forth from the Lord's presence and burned them up, and they died there before the Lord. Then Moses said to Aaron, "This is what the Lord meant when he said,

'I will display my holiness through those who come near me. I will display my glory before all the people."

And Aaron was silent" (Leviticus 10:1-3).

Brethren in CHRIST, the truth is that numerous characteristics of the Book of Leviticus seem far-off and odd to all of us believers today. One of the explanations is that we have never participated in animal sacrifice or abided by Jewish nutritional laws. Afterwards JESUS fulfilled the necessities of the Old Testament sacrificial method; we are no longer under it. Nonetheless, learning the law offers a richer understanding of GOD'S gift to us in JESUS CHRIST.

We need to explore the Book of Hebrews 10:1-18. Here, the Apostle Paul, the author of the Book of Hebrews, expressed joy in contrasting between the sacrifice of JESUS and the sacrificial arrangement outlined in the Book of Leviticus.

The Book of Leviticus is the third of Book of Prophet Moses the Prophet of "FIRE." He notes that the sacrifices in Leviticus always pointed further than themselves. As the Book of Hebrews teaches, "it is unmanageable that the blood of bulls and goats to take away sins" (verse 4). But CHRIST JESUS, through HIS once-for all sacrifice, cleansed us from sin and made us holy (verse 10). Instead of having a priest, present offerings day after day, CHRIST fully attained our atonement for sin (verse 11). After HIS

Resurrection, JESUS is sitting at the right hand of HIS FATHER. JESUS WORK WAS COMPLETE (verse 12). When we trust in CHRIST death, to atone for our sin we receive forgiveness and are made holy (verse 14). Even more astounding, the HOLY SPIRIT OF GOD dwells inside of us. GOD'S presence is now not screened behind the veil in HOLY OF HOLIES. We have access to the FATHER of the entire Universe!

CHRIST'S Sacrifice Once For All:

The old system under the law of Moses was only a shadow, a dim preview of the good things to come, not the good things themselves. The sacrifices under that system were repeated and again, year after year, but they were never able to provide perfect cleansing for those who came to worship. 2 If they could have provided perfect cleansing, the sacrifices would have stopped, for the worshipers would have been purified once for all time, and their feelings of guilt would have disappeared. 3 But instead, those sacrifices reminded them of their sins year after year. 4 For it is not possible for the blood of bulls and goats to take away sins. 5 That is why, when CHRIST came into the world, he said to God, "You did not want animal sacrifices or sin offerings. But you have given me a body to offer. 6 You were not pleased with burnt offerings or other offerings for sin.

{ Jesus told him, "I am the way, the truth, and the life. No one can come to the Father except through me (John 14:6) }

7 Then I said, 'Look, I have come to do your will, O God as is written about me in the Scriptures." **8** First, Christ said, "You did not want animal sacrifices or sin offerings or burnt offerings or other offerings for sin, nor were you pleased with them" (though they are required by the law of Moses). **9** Then he said, "Look, I have come to do your will." He cancels the first covenant to put the second into effect. **10** For God's will was for us to be made holy by the sacrifice of the body of Jesus Christ, once for all time. **11** Under the old covenant, the priest stands and ministers before the altar day after day, offering the same sacrifices repeatedly, which can never take away sins. **12** But our High Priest offered himself to God as a single sacrifice for sins, good for all time. Then he sat down in the place of honor at God's right hand. **13** There he waits until his enemies are humbled and make a footstool under his feet. **14** For by that one offering he forever made perfect those who are being made holy.

15 And the Holy Spirit also testifies that this is so. For he says, **sixteen** "This is the new covenant I will make with my people on that day, says the Lord: I will put my laws in their hearts, and I will write honor at God's right hand. 13 There he waits until his enemies are humbled and made a footstool under his feet then on their minds." **17** Then he says, "I will never again remember their sins and lawless deeds." **18** And when sins have been forgiven, there is no need to offer any more sacrifices (Hebrews 10:1-18).

In conclusion, GOD, our HEAVEN FATHER, loves us immeasurably. HIS utmost gift to human race, HIS SON, JESUS CHRIST, reflects that love. "For God so loved the world that He gave His only begotten Son, that whoever believes in Him should not perish but have everlasting life (John 3:16 NKJV). This means that GOD'S love and HIS plan is for the happiness of His children. HE sent HIS SON JESUS CHRIST. GOD recognized that this life would be full of trials and insecurity. HE knew that we would fall short and make mistakes. So, HE sent HIS SON, JESUS CHRIST, to earth. THE GLORY OF ISRAEL; CHRIST JESUS lived a perfect, and sinless life. HE taught HIS gospel and presented to us the right way to live. CHRIST willingly gave HIS own life as a sacrifice for our sins. HE IS OUR LOVING SAVIOR, REDEEMER, THE LION OF THE TRIBE OF JUDAH and HEAVEN'S TREASURE. If you are feeling overwhelmed, it is continuously good to devote time to prayer. Ask your HEAVENLY FATHER for HIS divine guidance in your life. Ask HIM to use the truth of HIS WORD to minister into your situation.

> **Jesus told him, "I am the way, the truth, and the life. No one can come to the Father except through me (John 14:6)**

CHAPTER 14

LIVING A CHRIST-CENTERED LIFE!

In the world in which we live in today, is placing excessive pressure on GOD fearing people everywhere to lower or even abandon their values of virtuous living. On the other hand, despite the evils and temptations that surround us each day, we can and will find real joy today in living a CHRIRST-CENTEED life. Centering our lives in JESUS CHRIST and HIS gospel will bring steadiness and contentment to our lives, as the subsequent examples illustrate. The world in which we live is like the potter's spinning wheel, and the rapidity of that wheel is increasing. Comparable to the clay on the potter's wheel, we must be centered as well. Our fundamental the center of our lives, must be JESUS CHRIST and HIS gospel. Living a CHRIST-CENTERED life means we learn about JESUS CHRIST and HIS gospel and then we follow HIS example and keep HIS commandments with accuracy. The famous Prophet Isaiah stated, "But now, O Lord, thou art our father; we are the clay, and thou, our potter; and we all are the work of thy hand." If our lives are centered in JESUS CHRIST, HE can successfully mold us into who we need to be. We need to come back to HIM, and HIS HEAVENLY FATHER'S presence in the celestial KINGDOM. The joy we experience in this life will be in direct amount to how well our lives are centered on the teachings, for instance, and compensating sacrifice of JESUS CHRIST.

This learning makes known to us to the concept of positional truth. Positional truth has to do with who we are in CHRIST as believers. Since it has to do with who we are in CHRIST, it will also affect our self-concept. The focus nevertheless is on who we are in the SAVIOR through faith in HIM and how that should impact our lives as believers. We must understand that the first key to effectiveness in living a godly life is to know what GOD has done for us. This forms the foundation for our answer. Only as we understand and rest in how GOD has acted in CHRIST are we able to act through CHRIST. In terms of all aspects of our salvation and all that it brings we must know and consider that GOD has done it all. For instance, in Romans 12:3 we are told to think properly about who we really are according to God's grace. The method for knowing who we are, so that such knowledge transforms our motives and thinking is a renewed mind in the Word (12:2).

{
**But seek first the kingdom of God and
His righteousness, and all these things
shall be added to you (Matthew 6:33)**
}

As human beings who are spiritually weak, we not only need a proper self-concept we need God's power and ability to change and overcome the sinful nature (the flesh) and those patterns of life that are so damaging to ourselves and to others. The Christian's place in CHRIST and his co-identification with CHRIST in HIS death, burial, and resurrection form the foundation for victory over the flesh and a new capability for life. To be sure, the SPIRIT OF GOD, whose duty it is to glorify CHRIST and mediate HIS life to you and me, will never produce spiritual power or bring true spiritual change into any life that is not resting in the merit, significance, and abundance of CHRIST as the source and ground of all life and meaning. Such would be out of the question due to the purpose of the ministry of the Spirit as declared in Scripture. If we want to experience the transformed life, we must understand who we are in Christ by God's grace and how that affects our walk-in life. Understanding the practical ramifications of our position and union in Christ (Romans 6) is foundational to the walk in and by the Spirit of God (Romans 8). "Therefore I exhort you, brothers, and sisters, by the mercies of God, to present your bodies as a sacrifice alive, holy, and pleasing to God which is your reasonable service. 2 Do not be conformed to this present world, but be transformed by the renewing of your mind, so that you may evaluate and approve what is the will of God what is good and well-pleasing and perfect. 3 For by the grace given to me I say to every one of you not to think more highly of yourself than you ought to think, but to think with sober discernment, as God has distributed to each of you a measure of faith" (Romans 12:1-3).

Romans 12:4-9; For just as in one body we have many members, and not all the members serve the same function, five so we who are many are one body in Christ, and individually we are members who belong to one another. 6 And we have different gifts according to the grace given to us. If the gift is prophecy, that individual must use it in proportion to his faith. 7 If it is service, he must serve; if it is teaching, he must teach; 8 if it is exhortation, he must exhort; if it is contributing, he must do so with sincerity; if it is leadership, he must do so with diligence; if it is showing mercy, he must do so with cheerfulness. 9 Love must be without hypocrisy. Abhor what is evil, cling to what is good. An accurate and biblical self-concept has two important sides or contrasts. It contains both strength and humility. It contains both a deep concern over the fact of our sin and joy and relief over forgiveness, and both an intense sense of our inadequacy and need of God with an understanding of how God in grace has perfectly met that need in Christ.

Apostle Paul wrote in Colossians 2:6-12; Therefore, just as you received Christ Jesus as Lord, continue to live your lives in Him, seven rooted and built up in him and firm in your faith just as you were taught, and overflowing with thankfulness. 8 Be careful not to allow anyone to captivate you through an empty, deceitful philosophy that is according to human traditions and the elemental spirits of the world, and not according to Christ. 9 For in him all the fullness of deity lives in bodily form, ten and you have been filled in him, who is the head over every ruler and authority. 11 In him you also were circumcised—not, however, with a circumcision performed by human hands, but by the removal of the fleshly body, that is, through the circumcision done by Christ. 12 Having been buried with him in baptism, you also have been raised with him through your faith in the power of God who raised him from the dead. "I have been crucified with Christ; it is no longer I who live, but Christ lives in me; and the life which I now live in the flesh I live by faith in the Son of God, who loved me and gave Himself for me" (Galatians 2:20). 15 Love not the world, neither the things that are in the world. If any man loves the world, the love of the Father is not in him. 16 For all that is in the world, the lust of the flesh, and the lust of the eyes, and the pride of life, is not of the Father, but is of the world. 17 And the world passeth away, and the lust thereof: but he that doeth the will of God abideth for ever" (1st John 2:15-17).

> **But seek first the kingdom of God and His righteousness, and all these things shall be added to you (Matthew 6:33)**

Brothers and sisters, we need to be careful not to permit anyone to hypnotize you through a blank, deceitful attitude that is according to human customs and the essential spirits of the world, and not according to CHRIST. Satan is a master of deception, father of all liars and, aided by his world system in which we live and by our individual blindness, Satan trails (as he did with Adam and Eve in the beginning) to hold us incarcerated as slaves to a complete range of false beliefs and tactics by which we try to achieve that which our HEAVENLY FATHER only can give. Tragically, we seek to attain by our own self-effort that which we previously have in CHRIST. The consequence is we frequently become focused on false objectives which, like a compelling spell, hold us captive and keep us from encounter GOD'S love, strong point and independence and the significance of life in CHRIST. These goals we so often pursue involve standards of achievement we (or others) have established as evidence of our success and thus of our self-worth.

If each one of us is to live CHRIST Centered life or CHRIST like life, we must all endeavor with everything we have within our power to become as HE is. This sacred endeavoring involves coming to know the SAVIOR with HIS divine attributes. We must advance the capability to think, feel in addition to do as the SAVIOR would as we face our earthly knowledge. Is it possible for imperfect people like us living a CHRIST-LIKE Life? Let us look at what the SWORD OF THE SPIRIT SAY?

- ❖ We need to understand that GOD has a Purpose for Our Lives
Paul tells us in Romans 8:28 that all things work together for a "purpose" for
Committed to God. In Galatians 1:15-16 Paul tells us that he wasted no
time in fulfilling the purpose that Christ had for his life, and we are to do the same.
- ❖ We must recognize that Compliance always brings a blessing JESUS.
tells us in John 14:23 that our father loves obedience. When Saul disobeyed
God and tried to offer a sacrifice to pay for his willful disobedience; Samuel tells.
Saul in 1 Samuel 15:22 that obedience is better than sacrifice. And Psalm 37:4-5
us that if we "commit our ways" to the Lord and he shall give us the desires.
of our hearts.
- ❖ As supporters of JESUS CHRIST, we have two missions - Matthew 28:19-20.
Colossians 3:12-17; The first is the Great Commission. The second is living every day for JESUS CHRIST.

In summary for living a CHRIST Like life or CHRIST Centered life; Everyone has the choice to live his/her life in Scriptural traditional values to a specific individual who is his/her mentor. There is compensation for every method of life, one or the other good or bad a person decides on to live. For instance, King Hezekiah lived a David-like live which please the LORD; 2nd Chronicle 29:2, but some Kings like Zimri, and greedy King Ahab the husband of wicked Jezebel lived a Jeroboam-like life which was evil in the sight of the Lord 1Kings 16:18-18, 30. God wants all of us to live a life that is CHRIST- Centered life which the world can read, feel, perceive and distinguish that CHRIST truly lives in us. If we do this, from now on, the world will be drawn near unto HIM for SALVATION and deliverance.

> **But seek first the kingdom of God and His righteousness, and all these things shall be added to you (Matthew 6:33)**

CHAPTER 15

THE FEAR OF GOD IS A VEHICLE TO HEAVEN

Brothers and sisters for us to know that we are true created beings, we must know who the CREATOR is, what the purpose of man's creation is for; how to convey the tasks of a created being and how to reverence, the LORD of all creation. We must comprehend, grasp, distinguish, and care for the CREATOR'S purposes, desires, and demands and necessity act in harmony with the way of the CREATOR- fear GOD and avoid evil. I believe that fearing GOD does not require a force. It comes from inside of us. The Scripture says that HE created us for HIS pleasure. If our life does not bring pleasure to GOD, then the purpose for which HE created us is not beneficial to HIM. GOD gave us a free –will reverence HIM and not by force. We have choice to choose whom we will follow or whom we will honor and reverence while here in this earth: "The fear of the Lord is the beginning of wisdom: and the knowledge of the holy is understanding" (Proverbs 9:10).

Why Is It Significant To Fear GOD?

To fear our HEAVENLY FATHER and our CREATOR, is to reverence, honor, trust, appreciation, caring, submission, sanctification, love, along with unconditional and accepting worship, something given in return and submission. Disadvantaged of genuine understanding of GOD, humankind will not have sincere respect, honest trust, truthful concerned, sincere caring or submission. But only doubt, misunderstanding, dodging, and avoidance; without honest knowledge of GOD; Humankind will not have sincere sanctification and requital. And without genuine understanding of GOD, humanity will not have unpretentious worship and surrender. But only blind worship and misunderstanding without genuine knowledge of GOD; Humanity may not act in harmony with the way of GOD, or fear GOD, or turn away after evil. On the other hand, every activity and conduct in which man engages will evil. According to (Oswald Chambers), he states that "The amazing thing about fearing GOD is that when you fear GOD you fear nothing else." The Bible urges us to fear GOD.

> **God is to be feared in the assembly of the saints,**
> **And to be held in reverence by all *those* around Him**
> **(Psalm 89:7)**

Brothers and sisters, we have ALL-POWERFUL and HOLY GOD. HE holds the entire universe in HIS HANDS. We are part of the universe. That means that GOD is more than able of intensely changing any and every single part of our being. That is a complete foundation for fearing HIM. It is the same fear that we have when there is danger, for example a storm or uncontrolled car. These things can vividly affect your comfort and it is appropriate and intelligent to fear them. But GOD has also revealed HIMSELF to be faithful, caring, loving, and forgiving. Our fear for GOD should have this coating to it, also. Not only should we fear GOD, but because HE is the ALPHA AND OMEGA; MIGHTY CREATOR and is HE who holds our fate in HIS HANDS. But then again, we should likewise fear GOD in the sense that we do not want to mess up our relationship with HIM. The WORD OF GOD says that we can grieve GOD with our immoral choices. Just like we would fear hurting the people in our life who care about us, we should fear doing something that will negatively affect our relationship and connection with this affectionate, faithful, and kind GOD.

Having an appropriate reverence and holy respect for GOD is the beginning point for all true understanding about spiritual realities. "It is a dreadful thing to fall into the hands of the living God" (Hebrews 10:31). GOD to be feared does not mean to be fearful of GOD. That paints a picture of GOD as being harsh and scary. Fearful in the original Greek means profound respect or admiration. It means reverence with an attitude of humility. What GOD says to you should be heard and not pushed away. Listening to HIM through one's integrity and responding suitably is one who has the fear of the LORD.

Requiring actual trust in GOD, humankind will really know how to follow GOD and depend on HIM. It is only with real trust in and dependence on GOD; can people have honest thoughtful and understanding; together with real comprehension of GOD comes actual caring for HIM; only with genuine caring for GOD can human race have sincere obedience; only with genuine obedience to GOD can people have genuine sanctification. And only with genuine consecration to GOD can humanity have requital that is total and short of criticism. It is only with sincere trust and dependency, sincere understanding and caring, genuine obedience, genuine consecration and requital, can humanity truly come to know GOD'S temperament and spirit and to know the identity of the CREATOR; It is only when humankind have truly come to know the CREATOR can human race awaken in themselves genuine worship and submit; simply when they have real worship for and surrender to the CREATOR will humanity be able truly to put aside their evil ways, that is to say, to avoid evil. The fear of GOD is the uppermost remedy in contradiction of the fear of man. "The fear of the Lord is the beginning of knowledge: but the fools despise wisdom and instruction" (Proverbs 1:7).

This establishes the complete process of "fearing GOD in addition of exclusion evil," and is also the content in its total of fearing GOD and shunning evil, as well as the path that must be traversed to arrive at fearing GOD and avoiding evil.

Brothers and sisters, fearing GOD should be like the air we breathe every day of our life. And avoiding evil and knowing GOD in spirit and in truth are indivisibly related by countless threads, and the link among them are undeniable. If one wishes to attain to barring evil, one must first have real fear of GOD. If individual wishes to attain to real fear of GOD, everyone must first have real understanding of GOD; if one wishes to attain to knowledge of GOD, one must first experience GOD'S words, enter the reality of GOD'S words, experience GOD'S humbling and discipline, HIS discipline and judgment. If anyone wishes to experience GOD'S WORDS, one must first come face to face with GOD'S WORDS that is (Clinging to GOD), come face to face with GOD, and beg GOD to provide occasions to experience GOD'S WORDS in the method of all sorts of environments linking people, events, and objects. "And his mercy is for those who fear him from generation to generation" (Luke 1:50). If one wishes to come face to face with GOD and with GOD'S WORDS, individuals must first possess a humble and honest heart, readiness to accept the truth, the willingness to tolerate suffering.

**God is to be feared in the assembly of the saints,
And to be held in reverence by all *those* around Him
(Psalm 89:7)**

The determination and the courage to reject evil and the ambition to become a sincere created creature; "The fear of the LORD is a fountain of life that one may turn away from the snares of death" (Proverbs 14:27). In this way, going forward step by step, you will draw near to GOD, your heart will grow ever purer, and your life and the importance of being alive will, along with your familiarity of GOD, become ever more significant and wax ever healthier. "And he said to man, 'Behold, the fear of the Lord, which is wisdom, and to turn away from evil is understanding" (Job 28:28). Until, one day, you will feel that the CREATOR is no longer a question that the CREATOR has never been out of sight from you, that the CREATOR has never hidden HIS face from you, that the CREATOR is not at all far from you, that the CREATOR is no longer the ONE that you constantly long for in your thoughts but that you cannot reach with your emotional state, that HE is really and truly standing protector to your left and right, providing your life, and regulatory your destiny.

GOD is not on the remote prospect, nor has HE secreted HIMSELF high up in the clouds. HE is right by your side, presiding over your all, HE is everything that you have, and HE is the only thing you have. "And now, Israel, what does the Lord your God require of you, but to fear the Lord your God, to walk in all his ways, to love him, to serve the Lord your God with all your heart and with all your soul" (Deuteronomy 10:12 ESV). Such a GOD allows you to love HIM from the heart, cling to HIM, hold HIM close, admire HIM, fear to lose HIM, and be unwilling to renounce HIM any longer, and refuse to comply to HIM any longer, or any longer to avoid HIM or put HIM at a Distance. "The fear of the Lord is hatred of evil. Pride and arrogance and the way of evil and perverted speech I hate" (Proverbs 8:13 ESV).

All you want is to care for HIM, obey HIM, requite all that HE gives you, and submit to HIS AUTHORITY. You no longer refuse to be guided, supplied, watched over, and kept by HIM, no longer refuse what HE commands and ordains for you. All you want is to follow HIM, walk together with HIM to HIS left or right, all you want is to accept HIM as your one and only in this life, to accept HIM as your one and only LORD, your one and only GOD ALMIGHTY. "The end of the matter; all has been heard. Fear God and keep his commandments, for this is the whole duty of man" (Ecclesiastes 12:13 ESV).

{
God is to be feared in the assembly of the saints,
And to be held in reverence by all those around Him
(Psalm 89:7)
}

CHAPTER 16

MUST WE CONTINUE IN SIN THAT GRACE MAY ABOUND?

At the end of Romans 1-5 Apostle Paul produced the most fundamental emphasis on justification by grace over faith, not together with works of the law. Paul one of the greatest teachers in the New Testaments taught (in Romans 5:18) that "as through one transgression of Adam there resulted condemnation to all men, even so through one act of righteousness of CHRIST there resulted justification of life to all men." In other words, our unification with Adam brought us condemnation because of his disobedience to GOD; and our coming together with CHRIST brings us justification because of HIS OBEDIENCE. This is extreme grace: CHRIST'S OBEDIENCE, not ours, is the ground of our justification GOD counts us righteous, and receives us, not because of performances done by us in righteousness (Titus 3:5), but because of actions done by CHRIST in righteousness (Romans 5:18). The complete point of getting Adam into the picture here at the end of Romans 1-5 is to make this drastically gracious way of justification perilously clear. We are doomed in Adam as his sin is accredited to us; we are justified in CHRIST as his righteousness is credited to us. TO GOD ALONE BE ALL THE GLORY FOR HIS LOVE FOR US THAT HE SENT HIS ONLY BEGOTTEN SON TO COME AND REDEEM US FROM THE SIN OF ADAM.

One Ultimate Problem In Life:

We are all saved, because we are united by faith in the direction of JESUS CHRIST, the second Adam. As we enter Romans chapter 6, we are captivated by one of the utmost issues in the Believers life. And that means one of the utmost issues in a lifetime period. Christian life is the only life that will lead us to eternal life. Consequently, what we are about to see is pertinent and crucial for every Tom, Dick, and Harry, whether they call themselves Christian or not. Jews, Muslims, Buddhists, Hindus, spiritualists, atheists, every person who rose from Adam needs to know what Apostle Paul was talking about in Romans 6. What Apostle Paul defines here is not provincial, narrow-minded, denominational, regional, or ethnic. It is relayed to everyone because it describes the only type of life that leads to everlasting life. Every one of us are sinners and guilt-ridden because we are united to the first man-Adam. And there is a kind of life that comes from being unified to CHRIST. That life leads to HEAVEN. And that is the only life we talk about. That is what was at stake in Romans **6.**

> Therefore, as through one man's offense judgment came to all men, resulting in condemnation, even so through one Man's righteous act the gift came to all men, resulting in justification of life. For as by one man's disobedience many were made sinners, so also by one Man's obedience many will be made righteous **(Romans 5:18-19)**

Dead to Sin, Alive to GOD:

What shall we say then? Shall we continue in sin that grace may abound? 2 Certainly not! How shall we who died to sin live any longer in it? 3 Or do you not know that as many of us as were baptized into Christ Jesus were baptized into His death? 4 Therefore we were buried with Him through baptism into death, that just as Christ was raised from the dead by the glory of the FATHER, even so we also should walk in newness of life. 5 For if we have been united together in the likeness of His death, certainly we also shall be in the likeness of His resurrection, 6 knowing this, that our old man was crucified with Him, that the body of sin might be a done away with, that we should no longer be slaves of sin. 7 For he who has died has been [b]freed from sin. 8 Now if we died with Christ, we believe that we shall also live with Him, nine knowing that Christ, having been raised from the dead, dies no more. Death no longer has dominion over Him. 10 For the death that He died, He died to sin once for all; but the life that He lives, He lives to God. 11 Likewise you also, [c]reckon yourselves to be dead indeed to sin, but alive to God in Christ Jesus our Lord. 12 Therefore do not let sin reign in your mortal body, that you should obey it in its lusts. 13 And do not present your members as [d]instruments of unrighteousness to sin but present yourselves to God as being alive from the dead, and your members as instruments of righteousness to God. 14 For sin shall not have dominion over you, for you are not under law but under grace (Romans 6:1-14 NKJV).

A Dead Person Cannot Sin?

I used to be a Baptismal director in my old Church. It was an experience indeed. During Baptismal class all the candidates were taught that this is a public declaration of one denouncing this world and to follow CHRIST. When you are immersed inside the water during baptism, you are now buried with CHRIST in HIS death and when you come out of the water you are now risen with CHRIST in HIS resurrection. It is important that we know this. Look at Romans 6:3; see what Apostle Paul says: "Or do you not know that as many of us as were baptized into Christ Jesus were baptized into His death?" (Romans 6:3; NKJV). After giving his summary explanation Dead men do not sin, he asks, "Do you not know?" Have you not been taught? Surely you know these things. Surely someone explained to you what your baptism means. In other words, Paul believes that this is important to know and that it is surprising when Christians do not know it. So, if we have been failed you in this area and not taught you this, let us grow now in the knowledge and the grace of our Lord Jesus Christ (2 Peter 3:18).

The explanation Paul gives for dead people not sinning can be summed up in three stages:

- As soon as CHRIST died, believers in some crucial common sense died in HIM and with HIM. "For if we have become united with Him in the likeness of His death" (Romans 6:5)

- The minute CHRIST rose, all Christians in some crucial senses were made alive in HIM.

- Consequently, believers are directed to turn out to be in practice what we are in CHRIST: dead to sin and alive to GOD.

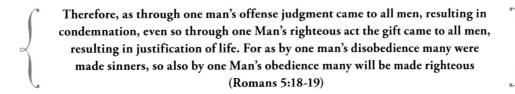

Therefore, as through one man's offense judgment came to all men, resulting in condemnation, even so through one Man's righteous act the gift came to all men, resulting in justification of life. For as by one man's disobedience many were made sinners, so also by one Man's obedience many will be made righteous (Romans 5:18-19)

In summary, when CHRIST died, believers in some critical sense died in HIM and with HIM. Romans 6:5, "For if we have become united with Him in the likeness of His death" (Romans 6:6, "Knowing this, that our old self was crucified with Him, in order that our body of sin might be done away with." (Romans 6:8). So, there is a union with Christ that makes what happened to him valid for us in him. When he died, we died. That is the key to why the justified do not go on sinning. We are justified by grace through faith alone because of our union with CHRIST whose righteousness is counted as ours. And now we see that this same union with Christ explains why we will not continue in sin. Brethren, we cannot continue in sin after we accepted CHRIST as our LORD AND SAVIOR. THE SWORD OF THE SPIRIT SAYS WE SHOULD BE HOLY BECAUSE OUR CREATOR IS HOLY. NO UNHOLY PERSON WILL INTER THE KINGDOM OF GOD.

{
Therefore, as through one man's offense judgment came to all men, resulting in condemnation, even so through one Man's righteous act the gift came to all men, resulting in justification of life. For as by one man's disobedience many were made sinners, so also by one Man's obedience many will be made righteous (Romans 5:18-19)
}

CHAPTER 17

GOD IS NOT A RESPECTER OF PERSONS

GOD honors HIS WORD more than anything else. Our GOD is not respecter of any persons! From the foundation of this world till this moment, from Lucifer, Adam and Eve, Moses, Aron, Miriam, King Saul, King David, and King Solomon. Personally, I see all these interactions from the people with as not obeying GOD. GOD will not lower HIS standard for any man. When the Bible says to us that GOD is not partial, it means that HE does not bend or ignore HIS standards for certain individuals. A mutual experience in every single country is that the rich, powerful, and politically connected are favored, but the common person is not. The rich, famous escape prison but not the average person. But that is not the case with GOD. When our HEAVENLY FATHER sent HIS SON to come to the world to redeem humanity, HE did not just send CHRIST to die for the rich and famous, (celebrity). GOD does not see the social class or those with economic advantages. HE has open hands and an open mind. All that GOD requires from us is simple obedience. GOD impartially saves everyone who believes in JESUS CHRIST. They do not have to do any decent work to go to HEAVEN. Salvation is by grace alone, through faith alone and in CHRIST alone. This idea that God is not a respecter of persons, is not partial, toward people is a theme throughout the Scripture. And God instructs us that we should not be partial to people, but always judge rightly.

GOD WILL NEVER LOWER HIS STANDARDS FOR ANYONE!
MOSES:

Moses is regarded as the greatest Prophet in the Nation of Israel and in the Bible. GOD had called Moses from the land of Midian to return to Egypt and lead the Hebrew people out of slavery; after Moses ran for his life from the then king Pharaoh's plot to kill him because of his action against Egyptian person trying to fight with an Israeli. Moses encounters GOD in a burning bush. GOD told Moses that HE had heard the cry of HIS people and their afflictions. GOD wants Moses to go back to Egypt to take HIS people out of Egypt. After some preliminary objections, Moses accepted the will of GOD, packed up his family, and started his journey west (Egypt). "Then something strange and troubling happened. 24 And it happened on the way, at the encampment, that the Lord met him and sought to kill him. 25 Then Zipporah took a sharp stone and cut off the foreskin of her son and cast it at Moses' feet, and said, "Surely you are a husband of blood to me!" 26 So He let him go. Then she said, "You are a husband of blood!" because of the circumcision (Exodus 4:24-26 NKJV).

> **Therefore you shall be perfect, just as**
> **your Father in heaven is perfect**
> **(Matthew 5:28)**

Based on the circumstance that GOD was going to kill Moses, it is assumed that Moses had committed some sin against GOD. The fact that the circumcision of Moses' son caused the LORD to concede shows that Moses' sin was a failure to circumcise his son. The fact that Moses's wife Zipporah, not Moses, did the surgical procedure proposes that Moses was incapable of doing it himself; the same assumption is maintained by the fact that Zipporah touched Moses' feet with the proof of circumcision this would be more natural if Moses were incapacitated. And, if Moses was confined to bed, the method that GOD was using to kill him was a sickness of some kind. Consequently, as far as we can tell, GOD was intimidating to kill Moses because Moses had not circumcised his son. The question then is why was that specific sin being judged so severely? With conviction, there were other sins that Moses was guilty of, yet GOD chose to follow the death consequence over a lack of circumcision. The answer goes back to the time of GOD'S friendship with Abraham, the father of the Jewish people. This is particularly important to GOD, because this is integral part of the covenant HE made with Abraham.

GOD CAN NOT LOWER HIS STANDARDS:

Most of us at some point in our life lower our standards, self-respect, and goods to get ahead or to select a mate. Most updated churches have done so, which is contrary to the Scripture. But then again, no matter what, GOD never lowers HIS standards to put up with us nor is HE willing to agree to take less than the best from us. Most people think that because they go to Church or participate in Church events that they are, without a doubt, on their way to HEAVEN. IT IS NOT SO BROTHERS AND SISTERS. SIN STINKS BEFORE GOD. HE NEVER LOWERS HIS STANDARD FOR ANYONE; NO MATTER WHO YOU ARE. If GOD DID NOT LOWER HIS STANDARD FOR MOSES, THE GREATEST PROPHET IN THE WHOLE UNIVERS HE WILL NOT DO IT FOR YOU OR ME. WE NEED TO BE CLEAR ON THIS? Our HEAVELY FATHER does not lower HIS standards to put up with HIS children. We HIS children need to raise our standards to please HIM. GOD standard is nothing but perfection. HIS standard is completely different from ours.

MOSES SECOND INCIDENT:
WAS IT ANGER OR DISOBEDINCE?

Personally that Moses was the greatest Israel Prophet. To me, Moses is like JESUS CHRIST the SAVIOR in the New Testament. Moses was called by GOD as a leader of the Exodus; He is the one true individual through whom GOD brought HIS people from Egyptian slavery. GOD entrusted the Law to Moses. OUR LORD JESUS demonstrated that Moses foretold His own work as the Messiah (John 3:14–15). As a believer, it will be a grave mistake not to seriously consider what happened to Moses at verge of his breakthrough in leading the children of Israel to the Promised Land that the LORD had promised them. In Deuteronomy 34 we read that GOD HIMSELF buried Moses. We are also told that, "since then, no prophet has risen in Israel like Moses, whom the Lord knew face to face. For no one has ever shown the mighty power or performed the impressive deeds that Moses did in the sight of all Israel" (Deuteronomy 34:10, 12). Yet Moses, for all his blessings, was not allowed to enter the Promised Land. But why?

> { **Therefore you shall be perfect, just as your Father in heaven is perfect (Matthew 5:28)** }

In Deuteronomy 32:51–52 God gives the reason that Moses was not permitted to enter the Promised Land: "This is because you broke faith with me in the presence of the Israelites at the waters of Meribah Kadesh in the Desert of Zin and because you did not uphold my holiness among the Israelites. Therefore, you will see the land only from a distance; you will not enter the land I am giving to the people of Israel." GOD was true to HIS promise. HE showed Moses the Promised Land, but did not let him enter in. GOD WILL NEVER LOWER HIS STANDARD FOR ANYONE. This portion of the Scripture scared me to death. If Moses, the greatest Prophet in the whole wide world did not make it to promise land; then why do I think that I can disobey GOD and get away with it? It is impossible. GOD is not a respecter of any person. Moses went through a lot of challenges with the children of Israel right from the time they were leaving Egypt to the time he went to get the ten Commandments from GOD. The Bible even called the children of Israel stiff neck people.

WHAT DID MOSES DO?

The incident at the waters of Meribah Kadesh is recorded in Numbers 20. Nearing the end of their forty years of wandering, the Israelites came to the Desert of Zin. There was no water, and the community turned against Moses and Aaron. Moses and Aaron went to the tent of meeting and prostrated themselves before GOD. GOD told Moses and Aaron to gather the assembly and speak to the rock. Water would come forth. Moses took the staff and gathered the men. At that moment, in anger, Moses said to them, "Listen, you rebel, must we bring you water out of this rock?" Then Moses struck the rock twice with his staff (Numbers 20:10–11). Water came from the rock, as GOD had promised. But GOD immediately told Moses and Aaron that, because they failed to trust HIM enough to honor HIM as HOLY, they would not bring the children of Israel into the Promised Land (verse 12). Similarly, Moses took the credit for bringing forth the water. He questions the people at the rock, "Must we bring you water out of this rock?" (Numbers 20:10, emphasis added). Moses was taking credit for the miracle himself (and Aaron), instead of attributing it to God. Moses did this publicly. God could not let it go unpunished and expect the Israelites to understand His holiness. Brothers and sisters, it is not how we start a journey but how we end it is what really matters. May the LORD help us.

OBEDIENCE IS THE KEY IN SERVING GOD!

Moses took the credit for bringing forth the water. He asks the people gathered at the rock, "Must we bring you water out of this rock?" (Numbers 20:10). Moses was taking credit for the miracle himself (and Aaron), instead of attributing it to GOD. Moses did this publicly. GOD could not let it go unpunished and expect the Israelites to understand HIS HOLINESS. For us to meet GOD's standards, we must comply to Romans 12:1-2, which tells us to present our bodies as living sacrifices; holy and acceptable unto God which is our reasonable service and not to be conformed to this world but to be transformed by the renewing of our minds. That we may prove what is that good, acceptable and the perfect will of GOD. Do you know what the penalty of sin is? The Bible states in "The wage of sin is death, but the gift of God is eternal life through Jesus Christ our Lord" (Romans 6:23).

For there is no respect of persons with God. For as many as have sinned without law shall also perish without law: and as many as have sinned in the law shall be judged by the law; (Romans 2:11-12)

Most of us believers today, even Pastors, Bishops, Evangelist, Teachers, and other Ministers in GOD'S Vineyard will do the same thing Moses did. Let me take us back to Numbers 20:3-9; the children of Israel complained bitterly against Moses and Aron. 3 And the people contended with Moses and spoke, saying: "If only we had died when our brethren died before the Lord! 4 Why have you brought up the assembly of the Lord into this wilderness, that we and our animals should die here? 5 And why have you made us come up out of Egypt, to bring us to this evil place? It is not a place of grain, figs, vines, or pomegranates; nor is there any water to drink." 6 So Moses and Aaron went from the presence of the assembly to the door of the tabernacle of meeting, and they fell on their faces. And the glory of the Lord appeared to them. 7 Then the Lord spoke to Moses, saying, 8 "Take the rod; you and your brother Aaron gather the congregation together. Speak to the rock before their eyes, and it will yield its water; thus, you shall bring water for them out of the rock and give drink to the congregation and their animals." 9 So Moses took the rod from before the Lord as He commanded him. GOD'S instruction was for Moses to speak to the rock and, but Moses lifted his hand and struck the rock twice with his rod; (Verse 13) This was the water of Meribah, because the children of Israel contended with the LORD, and HE was hallowed among them. Could Moses have done this because of anger and frustration?

Opposition of Aaron and Miriam!

Are Aaron and Miriam Moses' siblings jealous of him? It seems to me that they were not pleased that their brother married a foreign woman. Then Miriam and Aaron spoke against Moses because of the Ethiopian woman whom he had married; for he had married an Ethiopian woman. 2 So they said, "Has the Lord indeed spoken only through Moses? Has He not spoken through us also?" And the Lord heard it. 3 (Now the man Moses was very humble, more than all men who were on the face of the earth.) 4 Suddenly the Lord said to Moses, Aaron, and Miriam, "Come out, you three, to the tabernacle of meeting!" So, the three came out. 5 Then the Lord came down in the pillar of cloud and stood in the door of the tabernacle and called Aaron and Miriam. And they both went forward. 6 Then He said, "Hear now My words: If there is a prophet among you, I, the Lord, make Myself known to him in a vision; I speak to him in a dream. 7 Not so with My servant Moses; He is faithful in all My house. 8 I speak with him face to face, even plainly, and not in dark sayings; And he sees the form of the Lord. Why then were you not afraid To speak against My servant Moses?" 9 So the anger of the Lord was aroused against them, and He departed. 10 And when the cloud departed from above the tabernacle, suddenly Miriam became leprous, as white as snow. Then Aaron turned toward Miriam, and there she was, a person with leprosy.

Judgment for Disobedience! (Nadab and Abihu)

GOD is not respecter of any person. Brethren, the only way to get right with GOD is by obeying HIM. How can a man that is created by GOD disobey HIM, challenge, and question GOD'S own authority? Many in the Scripture that did this also get what they deserve from GOD. HE only needs our unlimited loyalty to HIM. We saw how GOD dealt with all the above-mentioned individuals. Irrespective of our positions, our social status, we must reverence, obey, honor, and follow through with HIS instructions. We must serve HIM with our mind, heart, and soul.

 For there is no respect of persons with God. For as many as have sinned without law shall also perish without law: and as many as have sinned in the law shall be judged by the law; (Romans 2:11-12)

Why was it bad that Aaron and his sons burned the sin offering in Leviticus 10:16–20? In Exodus 30 and Leviticus, The LORD GOD Almighty outlined a proper sacrifice to HIM. Aaron, the chief priest, was to present all offerings on behalf of himself and the people. "Then Moses said to Aaron, "Approach the altar and present your sin offering and your whole burnt offering to make atonement for yourself. Then present the offerings to make atonement for the people, just as the LORD has commanded" (Leviticus 9:7). GOD would send HIS own fire to consume the sacrifice as a sign of HIS presence. First, Aaron's sons sinned in mortal terms. They exhibited self-importance, carelessness, or disregard. The story is consequently an ethics story, containing a worldwide moral lesson. Even if one does not believe in GOD, it is understandable that Aaron's sons deserved to be punished for a lack of following through with GOD'S instructions to the end.

The Sin of Nadab and Abihu!

According to the 3rd Book of Moses, Leviticus 10; Aaron's sons Nadab and Abihu put coals of fire in their incense burners and sprinkled incense over them. In this way, they disobeyed the LORD by burning before him the wrong kind of fire, different than he had commanded. ² So fire blazed forth from the LORD's presence and burned them up, and they died there before the LORD. ³ Then Moses said to Aaron,

"This is what the LORD meant when he said,
'I will display my holiness through those who come near me.
I will be glorified before all the people" (Leviticus 10:1-3 NLT).

Due to the disobedience of Aaron's sons Nadab and Abihu, the LORD instigated those two men to die. Later that day, Aaron and his remaining sons allowed the sin offering to burn up. Moses was angry with Aaron's other two sons, Eleazar and Ithamar, as a result. For one thing, Moses had just commanded Aaron and his remaining sons to eat the offering (Leviticus 10:12–14). When he discovered they had let it burn up, he was understandably upset. One more reason Moses was upset was perhaps that he feared a destiny like that of Nadab and Abihu would befall Aaron, Eleazar, and Ithamar. Due to their grief over the deaths of Nadab and Abihu, Aaron and his sons Eleazar and Ithamar chose to let the sacrifice burn up rather than to eat it.

Moses was upset because this was breaking the command GOD had given the priest to use this offering in part as their food. One more reason Moses was upset was perhaps that he feared a destiny like that of Nadab and Abihu would befall Aaron, Eleazar, and Ithamar. He confronted Aaron, saying, "Why didn't you eat the sin offering in the sanctuary area? . . . You should have eaten the goat in the sanctuary area, as I commanded" (Leviticus 10:17–18). Aaron's response to Moses is full of pathos: "Today my sons presented both their sin offering and their burnt offering to the LORD. And yet this tragedy has happened to me. If I had eaten the people's sin offering on such a tragic day as this, would the LORD have been pleased?" (Leviticus 10:19, NLT). These words satisfied Moses that Aaron was living in fear and obedience to God (verse 20).

This was a revelation for me, it is important to be careful in criticizing true men and women of GOD. GOD will surely fight their battle. The elder brother of Moses, Aron and his elder sister Miriam did not like the fact that Moses married an African woman from Ethiopian. Both questioned Moses "Has the LORD indeed spoken only through Moses? Has He not spoken to us also?" Please let us be incredibly careful how we talk about people of GOD.

 For there is no respect of persons with God. For as many as have sinned without law shall also perish without law: and as many as have sinned in the law shall be judged by the law; (Romans 2:11-12)

HOW TO GET RIGHT WITH GOD IS TO OBEY HIM!
Why Will David Take The Census?

GOD can use anyone the way HE wants. No one can question GOD. HE is a SOVERIGN GOD. HE IS all KNOWING GOD, UNLIMITED GOD, UNCHANGEABLE GOD, and ALL AND MIGHTY GOD. HE IS THE CREATOR OF THE WHOLE UNIVERSE. "Again the anger of the Lord was aroused against Israel, and He moved David against them to say, "Go, number Israel and Judah." 2 So the king said to Joab the commander of the army who was with him, "Now go throughout all the tribes of Israel, from Dan to Beersheba, and count the people, that I may know the number of the people" (2nd Samuel 24:1-2).

The similar account of the event adjoining the census, on the other hand, reveals it was Satan who provoked David to take the census: "Now Satan stood up against Israel, and moved David to number Israel. So David said to Joab and to the leaders of the people, "Go, number Israel from Beersheba to Dan, and bring the number of them to me that I may know it" (1st Chronicles 21:1-2 NKJV). This discrepancy is often clarified by the understanding that, to achieve HIS purposes, sometimes GOD sovereignly permits Satan to act. GOD can use Satan in numerous ways, with the outcome being the purifying, chastising, and refining of disobedient believers (Luke 22:31–32). This may have been the case with David. GOD permitted Satan to tempt him, and David sinned, revealing his pride, and GOD then dealt with David accordingly.

As per why GOD was annoyed at David, is because in those periods a man only had the right to tally or number what belonged to him. Israel does not belong to David; GOD owns Israel. Israel is HIS covenant children. HE cannot share HIS glory with any man. GOD is not respecter of anybody. We need to settle this fact in our heart. In Exodus 30:12 GOD told Moses, "When you take a census of the Israelites to count them, each one must pay the LORD a ransom for his life at the time he is counted. Then no plague will come on them when you number them." It was up to GOD to command a census, and if David counted, he should only have done it at GOD'S command, receiving a ransom to "atone" for the counting. This is why GOD was angry again with Israel and is also why David was "conscience-stricken" afterward he counted Israel. David knew it was wrong. "And David's heart condemned him after he had numbered the people. So David said to the Lord, "I have sinned greatly in what I have done; but now, I pray, O Lord, take away the iniquity of Your servant, for I have done very foolishly" (2 Samuel 24:10 NKJV).

The psalmist tells us, "As for God, His way is perfect" (Psalm 18:30). If God's ways are "perfect," then we can trust that whatever He does and whatever He allows is also perfect. Our responsibility to GOD is to OBEY HIM, to TRUST HIM, and to SUBMIT TO HIS WILL, whether we understand it or not. In conclusion, let us endeavor to obey GOD. Disobedience is sin. GOD is HOLY and so HE expects us to be HOLY. We cannot do it by our strength but by HIS grace and mercy it can be obtained by praying to HIM daily and Studying HIS WORD.

Do you really think that you can keep lying, committing fornication, cheating, and stealing then end up in heaven because of a good deed you did? Galatians 5:19-21 tells us that those who do such things shall not inherit the kingdom of God. Ephesians 2:8-9 says, "For by grace we are saved through faith not of ourselves, it is the gift of God not of works lest anyone should boast."

For there is no respect of persons with God. For as many as have sinned without law shall also perish without law: and as many as have sinned in the law shall be judged by the law; (Romans 2:11-12)

In summary, I have explained Through the SWORD OF THE SPIRIT that when the Scripture says GOD is not a respecter of persons, this means HE does not ignore or change HIS standards for anyone. The Bible teaches that GOD knows our thoughts and, consequently, our hearts (Proverbs 15:11; 21:2; Matthew 9:4; Mark 2:8). From a human viewpoint, this is not the good news since GOD has a standard that everyone of us must adhere to go to HEAVEN. We cannot deceive GOD. HE IS GOD. HE IS OMINIPRESENT, OMNIPOTENT AND OMNISCIENCEGOD. When meeting with the gentile centurion Cornelius, the apostle Peter explained what God had revealed to him: "Of a truth I perceive that GOD is no respecter of persons: but in every nation he that feareth HIM, and worketh righteousness, is accepted with HIM" (Acts 10:34-35, KJV). The New King James Version translates "God is no respecter of persons" as "GOD shows no partiality."

 For there is no respect of persons with God. For as many as have sinned without law shall also perish without law: and as many as have sinned in the law shall be judged by the law; (Romans 2:11-12)

CHAPTER 18

HELL IS NOT FOR A MAN!

GOD Is Not Willing For Anyone To Go To Hell!

The love of GOD towards humanity is beyond measure. HE sent HIS only begotten SON to reconcile us to HIM. GOD is not willing for anyone to perish, but that all should come to repentance. In our present world today, people need a passport to travel outside their own motherland. Deprived of a passport, one cannot travel without restrictions to some foreign countries. This is accurate for anyone who wants to be in HEAVEN to spend eternity with CHRIST JESUS. You can never enter HEAVEN unless you have what is needed to enter GOD'S HOLY and everlasting dwelling place. Since GOD is HOLY, as well as hates all sin, HE cannot accept anyone into HEAVEN that lived a sinful life. This should make us to be sensitive to live a sinful life. Each one of us needs to pause and consider if we are acceptable to enter HEAVEN, for all of us must admit that we have sin.

This is similar if we want to be considered a candidate of HEAVEN after transiting from this world. The passport here is the HOLY SON OF GOD. JESUS IS OUR PASSPORT TO HEAVEN. HE died on the Cross as a criminal. HE took our place on the Cross to redeem us from hell fire. It is always imperative to study the Bible verses in context, and it is particularly true with 2nd Peter 3:9, which reads, "The Lord is not slack concerning his promise, as some men count slackness; but is longsuffering to us-ward, not willing that any should perish, but that all should come to repentance" (2nd Peter 3:9, KJV). The second half of the verse, "not willing that any should perish, but that all should come to repentance," is often used to contend against the doctrine of election.

If we are careful and unbiased to take a good look at GOD'S commandments, which comprises not lying, not stealing, not committing adultery, and honoring your father and mother, Every one of us must admit at some point that we all have failed to keep GODS righteous standards and are guilt-ridden sinners. If you are unquestionably not sure about whether you have sinned, may I bring it to our attention to help us understand what GOD says about our sins? HE said, "For everyone has sinned; we all fall short of God's glorious standard" (Rom 3:23). That means each one of us is guilty before GOD. No one can claim to be sinless and ready to enter HEAVEN our own. GOD does not desire anyone to perish. HE wants all of us to come to repentance. It has never been in GOD'S plan to send any man or women to hell fire but only to the devil and his agents.

 The Lord is not really being slow about his promise, as some people think. No, he is being patient for your sake. He does not want anyone to be destroyed, but wants everyone to repent (2 Peter 3:9)

Some persons have been persuaded that our decent work for instance, donating money to the Church, helping less privilege ones, or self-righteousness, going to Church, reading the Bible, praying etc., can make them to go to HEAVEN. The problem is that none of our good work can take away the guilt of our sin. The Bible teaches that salvation is based on our faith, and not on our good works. "GOD SAVED YOU BY HIS GRACE WHEN YOU BELIEVED. And none of us can take credit for this; it is a gift from GOD. Salvation is not a reward for the good things we have done, so none of us can boast about it" (Ephesians 2:8, 9). In the first place of the creation, GOD did not desire for sin to enter the world through the fall of Adam and Eve, yet HE allowed it. In fact, it was part of HIS SOVEREIGN plan. GOD did not desire HIS only begotten SON to be betrayed, viciously tortured, and executed, yet HE allowed it. This, too, was part of GOD'S SOVEREIGN plan.

If you want to go to HEAVEN, GOD has provided a way for you to be accepted. You need to have your sins forgiven, and washed away, through the BLOOD of JESUS CHRIST, so you can be accepted as a citizen of HEAVEN. With the first example that I gave in the first paragraph, when people want to travel to a foreign country, they would be restricted if there is any criminal history in their record. This is remarkable like going to HEAVEN, for we cannot enter Heaven with all our sins. OUR GOD IS HOLY. Without Holiness no man will see GOD. So, GOD sent JESUS, HIS SON, to die in our place, and receive our punishment for sin. "HE personally carried our sins in HIS body on the Cross so that we can be dead to sin and live for what is right. By HIS wounds you are healed" (1 Peter 2:24). By recognizing our sinfulness before GOD, and accepting JESUS' sacrifice as payment for our sins, we can have our sins forgiven. Salvation is very unassuming. The Bible says we must place our trust in JESUS CHRIST as LORD. "If you publicly openly declare that Jesus is Lord and believe in your heart that God raised Him from the dead, you will be saved" (Romans 10:9).

Apply for your passport now if you want to go to HEAVEN after this life? Then take this opportunity to give your life to JESUS CHRIS by living a righteous life. Accept the gift of salvation that GOD provided to you through HIS SON. "Believe in the Lord Jesus and you will be saved, along with everyone in your household" (Acts 16:31). You may ask Jesus to give you this salvation through prayer right now. It is not late to ask the LORD to the Lord for your life. But death it will be too lake. There is no repentance in the grave. There are ONLY two places you can spend eternity either in HEAVEN OR IN HELL! GOD is waiting to give more people the opportunity to repent. In the same way, God does not desire anyone to perish. He desires all to come to repentance. At the same time, GOD knows that not everyone will come to repentance.

It is indisputable that many will perish (Matthew 7:13–14). Then being a contradiction to 2 Peter 3:9, God's electing and drawing of some to salvation is evidence that He truly does not desire people to perish. Were it not for election and the effectual calling of God, everyone would perish (John 6:44; Romans 8:29–30). You could use the following prayer to help you but be sure the words are sincere from your own heart.

PRAYER: "Dear LORD JESUS CHRIST, I know that I am a sinner; I want you LORD to be the LORD of my life. I want to live for you for the rest of my life. I am sorry for all the wicked things I have done. Please forgive me for all my sins. Help me from this day forward to live in faith and obedience to you, my LORD. Thank you for giving your life for me, Amen."

 The Lord is not really being slow about his promise, as some people think. No, he is being patient for your sake. He does not want anyone to be destroyed, but wants everyone to repent (2 Peter 3:9)

CHAPTER 19

CHOOSING TO LIVE FOR CHRIST

How Do We Really Live for CHRIST?

What is the significance to really live for Christ? As the writer of this book, what does it take to live for CHRIST is a question every Christian needs to answer by individuals including me? How do we know if we are truly living for HIM? According to Apostle Paul in the book of Philippians, 1:21; "He was imprisoned in Rome, awaiting a death verdict for his gospel ministry. In this explicit text, Paul articulates one of the most quoted passages in the Bible. He says, "For to me, to live is Christ and to die is gain" (Philippians, 1:21). This verse is the major theme of this passage. What is the true meaning of "To live is CHRIST?" stated by Apostle Paul. The Apostle saw himself as no longer thriving he left his previous life in arrears, and now CHRIST was his life and CHRIST alone.

His life began when he became blind on his way to Damascus to arrest and kill CHRIST followers; but in the process, he himself became a follower of CHRIST. Far along in Philippians 3, he recounts all the former things he took pride in his Jewish background, following the law, and being a Pharisee, and however, he says he totaled it all manure all nothing for the sake of gaining Christ (v. 7-8). CHRIST was the start of his life and getting to know him more was the continuation of his life. In addition, dying would be gain because would mean abode in the unconstrained presence of CHRIST.

Is JESUS CHRIST in your life? Is the Messiah your day-to-day passion? Is HE your hope for the future? In the book of Philippians, we get the opportunity to educate ourselves, about one of the outstanding Apostles and a mature believer Paul. He is somebody we should imitate. According to 1st Corinthians 11:1, Paul declares, "Imitate me as I imitate Christ." We can be sure that what we see here in Paul is not just expressive of his feelings and knowledge while in jail, but it is also rigid. It is a challenge for us to develop into spiritual maturity. Paul speaks this far along in Philippians: "Join with others in following my example, brothers, and take note of those who live according to the pattern we gave you" (Philippians 3:17).

Apostle Paul trained them to follow his example, and that example was a life truthfully lived for CHRIST and CHRIST alone. What is your life? "Whereas you do not know what will happen tomorrow. For what is your life? It is even a vapor that appears for a little time and then vanishes away" (James 4:14 b). What is it for which you are really living? I ask myself this question all the time. Dorothy, what is it that I am looking for in this world? Is it success, wealth, comfort, or family? If so, you will not be able to say to die is gain, to die would really be the loss of all you are truly living for. "Therefore, submit to God. Resist the devil and he will flee from you. 8 Draw near to God and He will draw near to you. Cleanse your hands, you sinners; and purify your hearts, you double-minded" (James 4:7-8). In this text we will see five principles about how to really live for CHRIST.

**And I trust that my life will bring honor to Christ,
whether I live or die. For to me, living means
living for Christ, and dying is even better
(Philippians 1:21-22)**

The book of Philippians 1:19-26 explained to us how Apostle Paul lived for CHRIST? How can we put on these values to our lives so we can also truly live for CHRIST? To Really live for CHRIST, We Must Trust and Submit to GOD'S Plan for I know that through your prayers and the help given by the Spirit of Jesus Christ, what has happened to me will turn out for my deliverance (Philippians 1:19). In this passage, Paul states that, because of the prayers of the saints and the help given by the Spirit of Christ, what had happened to him would turn out for his deliverance. What does he mean by what has happened? Paul is here referring to his imprisonment for preaching the gospel and the criticism by the Christian detractors. For I know that through your prayers and the help given by the Spirit of Jesus Christ, what has happened to me will turn out for my deliverance.

I eagerly expect and hope that I will in no way be ashamed but will have sufficient courage so that now as always Christ will be exalted in my body, whether by life or by death. For to me, to live is Christ and to die is gain. If I am to go on living in the body, this will mean fruitful labor for me. Yet what shall I choose? I do not know! I am torn between the two: I desire to depart and be with Christ, which is better by far; but it is more necessary for you that I remain in the body. Convinced of this, I know that I will remain, and I will continue with all of you for your progress and joy in the faith, so that through my being with you again your joy in Christ Jesus will overflow on account of me. (Philippians 1:19-26).

Some observers have taken this viewpoint. He does say in verse twenty-five that he was "convinced that he would remain" with the Philippians. He was persuaded that it was not GOD'S WILL for him to die but to be set free and to continue his ministry to others. Paul could be devoted to this. Still, the fact that Paul proves some doubt in verse twenty-one of his outcome makes many believe he cannot be referring to deliverance from prison. Paul says in verse twenty-one, that his hope is that Christ will be glorified in his body by life or by death. Therefore, deliverance does not refer to being released from prison. Apostle Paul's liberation means that GOD would work everything out for his sanctification. The word deliverance can also be translated "salvation" (KJV). There is a salvation in the past tense when we accepted Christ and began to follow him, but there is also a progressive sense of salvation. Philippians 2:12-13 says, "Work out your salvation with fear and trembling for it is God works in us to will and do of his good pleasure."

This aspect of salvation is to be made in the image of CHRIST. The purpose of GOD of saving us is not just to enter heaven but similarly to be made into the image of HIS ONLY BEGOTTEN SON. And GOD uses all good things and sad things to make us into HIS IMAGE. This is the promise in According to the book of Romans 8:28-29, "And we know that in all things God works for the good of those who love him, who have been called according to his purpose. For those God foreknew he also predestined to be conformed to the likeness of his Son, that he might be the firstborn among many brothers" (Romans 8:28-29). What is the good thing that GOD promises for every believer? The purpose is for us to have the image of HIS SON JESUS CHRIST. That was the deliverance Apostle Paul was confident in. He was confident that he would look like Christ, and specifically that Christ would be glorified in him whether by life or death (v. 20).

**And I trust that my life will bring honor to Christ,
whether I live or die. For to me, living means
living for Christ, and dying is even better
(Philippians 1:21-22)**

The story of David, Job, Joseph the son of Jacob, Nadab and his brother Abihu should serve us as a fitting example that every believer should follow when we are faced with challenges of life. In case of King David, after he was chased out of his own kingdom by his son Absalom; David and his mighty men were walking away from the kingdom as exiles, and a man named Shimei began to curse David and throw stones at him (2 Samuel 16). David's mighty men became angry and asked, "Why are you allowing him to curse you, let us take off his head." But David replied, "No, let him curse for God has commanded him to curse. GOD will hear his cursing and repay me with good for the cursing I have received today" (2 Samuel 16:11-12). David trusted in God's plan for his life and that God was working everything for his good. In case of Job, So Satan went out from the presence of the LORD and afflicted Job with painful sores from the soles of his feet to the top of his head. Then Job took a piece of broken pottery and scraped himself with it as he sat among the ashes. His wife said to him, "Are you still holding on to your integrity? Curse God and die!" (Job 2:7-9).

The case of Joseph and his brothers! Joseph was one of Jacob's 12 sons. His father loved him more than any of the others and gave him a colored cloak. His brothers were jealous of him and sold him into slavery. He was sold by his brothers to Egypt out of jealousy, hate and eventually he became steward to Potiphar, one of Pharaoh's officials. Potiphar's wife also falsely accused him, and this landed him in prison. He eventually released from prison and became the second in command in Egypt. It is important to forgive others and continue to love and care about them. Encourage the children to be as forgiving as Joseph was to his brothers. There is power in forgiveness. Joseph forgave his brothers and moved on with his jumble life. It is the very promise we have as believers in Romans 8:28: "And we know that in all things God works for the good of those who love him, who have been called according to his purpose." We know God is working all things good and bad for our good. This was Paul's confidence. Everything was working out for his delivery. "To live is Christ" means to trust God's will for our lives.

In summary, Brethren, as you read this book, have it in mind that without CHRIST there is no life. Our life will not be fulfilled without JESUS CHRIST THE SON OF THE HIGHEST GOD. We need to always trust GOD'S WILL. No matter the circumstances that we face every day of our life. Sometimes, life is not fair, but GOD is just and fair to us through HIS gift of JESUS and HOLY SPIRIT. David, Job, and Joseph all trusted in the WILL OF GOD. In these three examples, see how GOD delivered them from circumstances. Also, Apostle Paul trusted in GOD'S SOVEREIGN PLAN. In fact, he was consumed with GOD'S SOVEREIGN PLAN. We see this with many men of GOD in Bible especially when confronted with suffering.

We noted that during CHRIST agony over two thousand years ago, He prayed a very touching and a powerful prayer. HE prayed for the WILL of GOD to be done in HIM fulfilling the mission which HE left HIS throne in HEAVEN. JESUS is our role model. We need to always pray THE WILL of GOD in every area of our life. In Luke 22:42 THE SON OF GOD prayed, "FATHER, IF THOU BE WILLING, REMOVE THIS CUP FROM ME; NEVERTHELESS, NOT MY WILL, BUT THINE, BE DONE" (Luke 22:42). "For I came down from heaven, not to do mine own will, but the will of his that sent me" (John 6:38). Are you trusting GOD'S plan for your life? LORD, if your plan means illness or infirmity like it was with Jacob; LORD, if your plan means loss of my wealth and health as Job; LORD, if your plan means being persecuted or martyred as many of the Old Testament Prophets and New Testament Disciples, LORD, may YOUR WILL be done.

And I trust that my life will bring honor to Christ, whether I live or die. For to me, living means living for Christ, and dying is even better (Philippians 1:21-22)

LORD, just allow me to be faithful in doing your WILL and plan in my life. This is a hard prayer to pray. But GOD is in Control. Obey GOD'S WILL in your life. In HEAVEN we will rest from our labor and our performances will follow us. We will be compensated for our deeds, and the benefits will continue throughout eternity. Brothers and sisters, I am personally excited for this glorious place called HEAVEN. To live for CHRIST means to labor here on earth to sweat, to discipline ourselves, to bear pain and lack of sleep for CHRIST, but at death it means to release the yoke. COME, LORD! COME! MARANATHA!

**And I trust that my life will bring honor to Christ,
whether I live or die. For to me, living means
living for Christ, and dying is even better
(Philippians 1:21-22)**

CHAPTER 20

FLESH AGAINST THE SPIRIT!

Living By The Power Of The Spirit!

Spirit and flesh have always been against each other right from the time of JESUS. The LORD spoke clearly to HIS disciples that "Spirit is willing, but flesh is weak. The flesh is always weak. A winner spirit is the main significant to a productive life in the KINGDOM of GOD. As Believers, the state of our spirit will govern the superiority of our life. If an individual gets born-again in addition to make JESUS the LORD of their life but flops to advance and uphold their spirit, they will fall short of the whole thing that GOD has called them to do. So, as CHRIST followers, it is important that we do everything needed to make sure that our spirits are strong. As Christians, we should try to develop The Winner Spirit in our lives. A Winner is one who victories, one who fights, one who has overpowered and beaten all rivals, one who is greater and has all the characteristics of a winner. Our spirits should be fighting the good fight of faith and experiencing victory over the opponent. Our spirits should be bigger than our thoughts and bodies moderately than been measured by them. Our spirits should have all the qualities of a winner. Our spirits should flawlessly represent all that our Master JESUS CHRIST was when HE walked the Earth and all that HE still is today. This is The WINNER Spirit.

The Winner Spirit:

In emerging a strong spirit, The WINNER Spirit, you must comprehend the "man's make up" According to Apostle Paul in 1st Thessalonians 5:23 says, "And the very God of peace sanctify you wholly: and I pray God your whole spirit and soul and body be preserved blameless unto the coming of our Lord Jesus Christ." We do not have a spirit, but rather we are a spirit. Our spirit man is the actual us. When you made JESUS the LORD of your life, your spirit is the part of you that was born again and reconstructed in GOD'S image. Every individual who walks the face of the Earth is a spirit-being. When we die, our body gets buried, but the spirit still exists. If they made JESUS the LORD of their life, they (their spirit) will spend eternity in HEAVEN. If a person died with making peace with the LORD JESUS CHRIST, they (their spirit) will spend eternity in Hell. Our spirit-man is the real man that will exist for all of time without end. If you are going to develop your spirit into The Winner Spirit, then it is imperative that you be familiar with the truth that you are a spirit.

{ The sinful nature wants to do evil, which is just the opposite of what the Spirit wants. And the Spirit gives us desires that are the opposite of what the sinful nature desires. These two forces are constantly fighting each other, so you are not free to conduct your good intentions (Galatians 5:17) }

There is therefore now no condemnation to those who are in Christ Jesus, who do not walk according to the flesh, but according to the Spirit. For the law of the Spirit of life in Christ Jesus has made me free from the law of sin and death. For what the law could not do in that it was weak through the flesh, God did by sending His own Son in the likeness of sinful flesh, on account of sin: He condemned sin in the flesh, that the righteous requirement of the law might be fulfilled in us who do not walk according to the flesh but according to the Spirit. For those who live according to the flesh set their minds on the things of the flesh, but those who live according to the Spirit, the things of the Spirit. For to be carnally minded is death, but to be spiritually minded is life and peace. Because the carnal mind is enmity against God; for it is not subject to the law of God, nor indeed can be. So then, those who are in the flesh cannot please God (Romans 8:1-8 (NKJV).

We Are In A Fight!

Brethren, we are in a battle in this world. We might not be able to see it; we may forget that it is there. But then again, the enemy would love nothing more than to begin our year off with discouragement and defeat, conveying fear and stress. Do not let him win. If you are a faithful believer who is living like CHRIST and having HIS mindset while here in this wicked and mysterious world, you will not go for long without coming across spiritual warfare difficulties and attacks he will throw your way. GOD prompts us in HIS WORD to stay alert of Satan's arrangements, to live alert in this world, and to stay close to GOD. HE arms us with THE SWORD OF THE SPIRIT, WHICH IS THE WORD OF GOD, to stand against the enemy's lies. He equips us with strength, wisdom, and discernment through HIS OWN SPIRIT to stay strong in the spiritual warfare battle. HE invites us to spend time in HIS PRESENCE, through prayer and worship, pressing in to know HIM more.

Life in the Spirit Differentiated with life in the flesh!

According to Apostle Paul in the book of Galatian 5:19-21; When you follow the desires of your sinful nature, the results are very clear: sexual immorality, impurity, lustful pleasures, 20 idolatry, sorcery, hostility, quarreling, jealousy, outbursts of anger, selfish ambition, dissension, division, 21 envy, drunkenness, wild parties, and other sins like these. Let me tell you again, as I have before, that anyone living that sort of life will not inherit the Kingdom of God. If all believers are sensitive to act under the leadership and power of the blessed SPIRIT, nevertheless we may not be autonomous from the stirs and oppositions of the immoral nature which remains in us; it shall not have dominion more than us.

CHRIST followers participate in a battle in which they desire that grace may obtain full and immediate victory. And those who wish therefore to give themselves up to be directed by the HOLY SPIRIT, are not underneath the law as a covenant of works, nor unprotected to its dreadful curse. Their hatred of sin and desires after holiness show that they have a part in the salvation of the gospel. The works of the flesh are many and manifest. And these sins will shut men out of HEAVEN. Up till now what numbers, calling them Christians, live in these, and say they hope for heaven! The fruits of the SPIRIT, or of the transformed nature, which we are to do, are named and as the Apostle Paul had named works of the flesh, not only upsetting to men themselves, but nurture to make them so to one another, so here he chiefly notices the fruits of the Spirit, which have a habit of to make Christians friendly one to another, and to make them happy.

 The sinful nature wants to do evil, which is just the opposite of what the Spirit wants. And the Spirit gives us desires that are the opposite of what the sinful nature desires. These two forces are constantly fighting each other, so you are not free to conduct your good intentions (Galatians 5:17)

The FRUITS OF THE SPIRIT show that the Spirit leads such. By relating the works of the flesh and fruits of the Spirit, we were instructed on what to avoid and compete against and what we are to treasure and encourage and this is the genuine carefulness and attempt of all Christians. "Sin does not now reign in their mortal bodies, so that they obey it" (Romans 8:5). It is essential that we set ourselves seriously to crush the deeds of the body, and to walk in the newness of life. We should not be desirous of vain-glory, or excessively wanting for the regard and ovation of men, not provoking, or envying one another, but seeking to bring forth more plentifully those good fruits, which are, through JESUS CHRIST, to the praise and glory of GOD. Paul stated in Galatian 5:16-17; "So I say, let the Holy Spirit guide your lives. Then you will not be doing what your sinful nature craves. 17 The sinful nature wants to do evil, which is just the opposite of what the Spirit wants. And the Spirit gives us desires that are the opposite of what the sinful nature desires. These two forces are constantly fighting each other, so you are not free to conduct your good intentions" (Galatian 5:16-17).

FATHER, when we feel like the people around us are our enemies, please remind us that our true enemies are not flesh-and-blood people, but unseen beings who are focused on leading us away from YOU to an eternity of pain, sorrow, everlasting doom, and suffering. Help us to face our struggles and difficulties in the present-day considering eternity and the invisible battle for our mind that will lead only to death and hell. Deliver us from these hidden adversaries and let us feel YOUR presence when we are feeling frail and downcast so we can endure and win. In JESUS'CHRIST Name, Amen. "For we are not fighting against flesh-and-blood enemies, but against evil rulers and authorities of the unseen world, against mighty powers in this dark world, and against evil spirits in the heavenly places" (Ephesians 6:12 NLT).

The Works of the Flesh

And I will be grieved because many of you have not given up your old sins. You have not repented of your impurity, sexual immorality, and eagerness for lustful pleasure."

"Idolatry," The meaning, is "an admiration or reverence for something else other than GOD. Idolatry, more specifically, is the worship of something created which is in direct opposition to the worship of the CREATOR HIMSELF. Originally, a physical idol helped visualize the god it represented but later people worshipped the physical object itself."

"Idolatry may be classified as follows: (1) the worship of lifeless objects, such as stones, trees, rivers, etc.; (2) of animals; (3) of the higher powers of nature, such as the sun, moon, stars; and the forces of nature, as air, fire, etc.; (4) hero-worship or of deceased ancestors; (5) idealism, or the worship of abstractions Paul has been encouraging believers to "walk in (by) the Spirit." The Holy Spirit is an important message for Paul, he mentions the Holy Spirit 8 times in this chapter (NKJV). The conclusion here is that every believer has the Holy Spirit living in them. And that those who are led by the Spirit are the children of God (Romans 8:14).

> The sinful nature wants to do evil, which is just the opposite of what the Spirit wants. And the Spirit gives us desires that are the opposite of what the sinful nature desires. These two forces are constantly fighting each other, so you are not free to conduct your good intentions (Galatians 5:17)

We are taught by the Spirit, comforted by the Spirit, anointed, regenerated, sanctified, filled, and sealed by the Spirit. Verse 19a: "Now the works of the flesh are evident". "When you follow the desires of your sinful nature, the results are very clear" (Galatians 5: 19 NLT). Paul here deals with the sins of the flesh; however, it is hardly necessary to point out these sins since they are "evident." They are in plain view and obvious to everyone. "When Paul says that the acts of the flesh are obvious, he does not mean that they are all committed publicly where they may be seen. Some are, some are not. Instead, he means that it is obvious to all that such acts originate with the sinful nature, and not with the nature given believers by God." "Paul is teaching us here that the works of the flesh are plainly visible so that fleshly behavior (often referred to as carnal behavior) is readily apparent to all observers. In other words, to use a Biblical analogy, 'a tree is known by its fruit,' (Luke 6:43-45) in this case carnal people are known by their works."

Here Apostle Paul listed sixteen "Works of The Flesh?"

Brothers and sisters, please take your time to go through these sixteen works of the flesh. It is imperative for us to study the WORD OF GOD and hide it in our hearts that we might not knowingly sin against HIM. Any Believer who are guilty of the listed works of the flesh will not inherit the KINGDOM OF GOD. May GOD help us to pay close attention to HIS WORD in JESUS MIGHTY NAME AMEN. Galatians 5: 19b-21a: "which are: adultery, fornication, uncleanness, lewdness, idolatry, sorcery, hatred, contentions, jealousies, outbursts of wrath, selfish ambitions, dissensions, heresies, envy, murders, drunkenness, revelries, and the like"

"Adultery," Is voluntary sexual intercourse between a married person and a person who is not their spouse. It is number 7 in the list of the ten Commandments: "You shall not commit adultery" (Exodus 20:14). This was a serious offense in the Old Testament, "If there is a man who commits adultery with another man's wife, one who commits adultery with his friend's wife, the adulterer and the adulterer shall surely be put to death. (Leviticus 20:10). Proverbs 6:32, "But the man who commits adultery is an utter fool, for he destroys his own soul." This Sin always causes grief and pain! The lights at the front door are bright and cheerful, they flash, "Come on in, this is fun!" This will make you feel good! Celebrate! A little bit cannot hurt you. You only go around once in life, grab all the gusto you can!" But the tunnel at the end is dark and bleak, and you will find there, broken homes, shattered lives, anxiety, depression, guilt, rejection, grief, and pain. This Sin causes pain to those closest to us, our wife, husband, mom, dad, children, pastor, and friends. The entertainment industry pictures adultery as just a natural event in life, but adultery is not funny! I have seen this sin tear up too many homes, leaving children grieving over the loss.

"Fornication:" It includes any sexual sin committed by unmarried people, illicit sexual intercourse in general, distinguished from adultery. Fornication referred to any excessive behavior or lack of restraint, but eventually became associated with sexual excess and indulgence, of every kind of extramarital, unlawful, or unnatural sexual intercourse. Biblically, fornication has a little wider definition. It can refer to prostitution or promiscuous behavior or indulging in unlawful lust by either sex. (1ˢᵗ Corinthians 7:2), "Nevertheless, because of sexual immorality, let each man have his own wife, and let each woman have her own husband." 1ˢᵗ Corinthians 6:18, "Flee sexual immorality. Every sin that a man does is outside the body, but he who commits sexual immorality sins against his own body."

The sinful nature wants to do evil, which is just the opposite of what the Spirit wants. And the Spirit gives us desires that are the opposite of what the sinful nature desires. These two forces are constantly fighting each other, so you are not free to carry out your good intentions (Galatians 5:17)

"Uncleanness," Is also translated "impurity" It is a state of moral impurity related to thought, action, or speech. The unclean person sees dirt in everything. Colossians 3:5 NLT, "So put to death the sinful, earthly things lurking within you. Have nothing to do with sexual immorality, impurity, lust, and evil desires. Do not be greedy, for a greedy person is an idolater, worshiping the things of this world."

"Lewdness," It means, absence of restraint, indecency, wantonness, outrageous conduct shocking to public decency, to be lustful and excessive indulgence in sensual pleasures. 2nd Corinthians 12:21 NLT, "Yes, I am afraid that when I come again, God will humble me in your mental qualities, such as justice. Greediness or covetousness is synonymous with idolatry because it places selfish desire above obedience to God. For examples, approbation of Movie and television stars, sports stars, and celebrities in general! Romans 1:21-23, "…because, although they knew God, they did not glorify Him as God, nor were thankful, but became futile in their thoughts, and their foolish hearts were darkened. Professing to be wise, they became fools, and changed the glory of the incorruptible God into an image made like corruptible man—and birds and four-footed animals and creeping things."

"Sorcery," It means one who prepares or uses magical remedies; It was used to describe the use of magic which often involved the taking of drugs. "Ancient sorcerers and oracles commonly used mind-altering drugs to induce their visions and healings. Revelation 18:23, "For your merchants were the great men of the earth, for by your sorcery all the nations were deceived." Revelation 9:21, "And they did not repent of their murders or their sorceries or their sexual immorality or their thefts."

"Hatred," means an extreme negative attitude that is the opposite of love and friendship. This also means hostility, expressing enmity which may be open or hidden, articulating deep-rooted hatred or incompatible hostility. Proverbs 10:12, Hatred stirs up strife, but love covers all sins." Proverbs 10:18 NLT, "Hiding hatred makes you a liar; slandering others makes you a fool."

"Contentions," in Greek is Eris meaning, wrangling, quarrels, strife, unbridled and unholy competition. "It is essentially the sin which places self in the foreground and is the entire negation of Christian love…" –Barclay. It is a characteristic of the unsaved.

"It refers to persistent contention, bickering, petty disagreement, and enmity. It reflects a spirit of antagonistic competitiveness that fights to have its own way, regardless of cost to itself or of harm to others. This is produced by a deep desire to prevail over others, to gain the highest prestige, importance, and recognition possible. Strife is characterized by self-indulgence and egoism. It has no place even for simple tolerance, much less for humility or love.," Romans 13:13,14, "Let us walk properly, as in the day, not in revelry and drunkenness, not in lewdness and lust, not in strife and envy. But put on the Lord Jesus Christ, and make no provision for the flesh, to fulfill its lusts."

"Jealousies," The meaning is to be hot, to boil. It is a good word which describes eagerness, earnestness, excited devotion, single-minded commitment, fervency, eager desire, or enthusiastic interest in pursuit of something, but it can take on a negative connotation when it describes a reaction which borders on extreme or obsessive. "In itself it means only warmth, ardor, zeal, but for a bad cause or from a bad motive, jealousy, envy, rivalry results." 1st Corinthians 3:3 NASB, "for you are still carnal." For where there are envy, strife, and divisions among you, are you not carnal and behaving like mere men"?

 The sinful nature wants to do evil, which is just the opposite of what the Spirit wants. And the Spirit gives us desires that are the opposite of what the sinful nature desires. These two forces are constantly fighting each other, so you are not free to carry out your good intentions (Galatians 5:17)

"Selfish ambitions," Refers to self-seeking, strife, contentiousness, extreme selfishness, rivalry, and those who seek only their own. It usually conveys the idea of building oneself up by tearing someone else down. Philippians 2:3 NLT, "Do not be selfish; do not try to impress others. Be humble, thinking of others as better than yourselves." James 3:14 NASB, "But if you have bitter jealousy and selfish ambition in your heart, do not be arrogant and so lie against the truth."

"Dissensions," It means in Greek word, exactly a standing not together which is a picture of dissension, discord, disunity, contention, division into opposing groups. The idea of dissension is disagreement which leads to discord. Dissension is strife that arises from a difference of opinion and stresses a division into factions (especially factions in early church). Romans 16:17 NLT, "And now I make one more appeal, my dear brothers, and sisters. Watch out for people who cause divisions and upset people's faith by teaching things contrary to what you have been taught. Stay away from them."

"Heresies:" Heresy is called heir in Greek word; and is based primarily on teaching something in opposition or that which contradicts the truth of the Word of God. Titus 3:10, 11 NLT, "If people are causing divisions among you, give a first and second warning. After that, have nothing more to do with them. For people like that have turned away from the truth, and their own sins condemn them." 2nd Peter 2:1, "But there were also false prophets among the people, even as there will be false teachers among you, who will secretly bring in destructive heresies, even denying the Lord who bought them, and bring on themselves swift destruction. And many will follow their destructive ways, because of whom the way of truth will be blasphemed." 2nd Timothy 4:3-4, "For the time will come when they will not endure sound doctrine, but according to their own desires, because they have itching ears, they will heap up for themselves teachers; and they will turn their ears away from the truth and be turned aside to fables."

"Envy," Is extremely dangerous. Remember Joseph and his brothers (Jacob's children). Is the expression of pain felt at the sight of someone else's success or happiness? To envy is to feel a resentful dissatisfaction provoked by the belongings, accomplishments, or wherewithal of another along with the desire to have for oneself something possessed by another. "Jealousy and envy are close in meaning, but nevertheless are expressive of different approaches, for jealousy makes us fear to lose what we possess, while envy creates sorrow that others have what we do not have. In other words, we are jealous of our own possessions, but we are envious of another man's possessions. Jealousy fears to lose what it has, while envy is pained at seeing another have it!"

"Murders," Murdering anybody is a sin of the flesh, The word "murders" means homicide, the Bible distinguishes between killing someone and murdering him. Murder is the premeditation taking the life of a human being illegally. The Commandment in Exodus 20:13 and Deuteronomy 5:17 could read, "You shall not commit murder." The Law demanded death for those who committed this crime. That is capital punishment for cold-blooded, premeditated murder.

{ **I say then: Walk in the Spirit, and you shall not fulfill the lust of the flesh (Ephesians 5:16)** }

"Drunkenness," This is intentional and habitual intoxication. One cannot control his or her action when intoxicated. "For some of you hurry to eat your own meal without sharing with others. As a result, some go hungry while others get drunk" (1 Corinthians 11:21 NLT). Ephesians 5:18 admonishes us, "And do not be drunk with wine, in which is dissipation; but be filled with the Spirit.

"Revelries," originally referred to a band of friends who accompanied a victor in a battle or a sporting event, singing praises to the victor. But the word deteriorated until it came to mean partying or a noisy, violent parade of half drunken partygoers who marched through the streets at night with torches and music in honor of Bacchus or some other deity. Galatians 5:21c "of which I tell you beforehand, just as I also told you in time past, that those who practice such things will not inherit the kingdom of God."

How do we mean when we say the flesh lusts against the Spirit mean?

Dear friends, when we state that the flesh lusts against the spirit, it connotes that these desires, to do what is appropriate and to do whatever is self-centered, self-gratifying, uncontrolled, or self-promoting, even if it looks righteous, fight in in another directions. Flesh and spirit pull against each other in opposing directions.

{
**I say then: Walk in the Spirit, and you
shall not fulfill the lust of the flesh
(Ephesians 5:16)**
}

CHAPTER 21

THE MANIFESTATION OF PRAISE & WORSHIP!

With my personal experience, Praising and Worshiping GOD leads to Spiritual Alertness. There is no doubt in my mind that Praising and Worshiping GOD makes us closer to GOD which will lead us to have KINGDOM mindset. This will also make us to be sensitive to the leadership of HOLY SPIRIT. The power of PRAISING AND WORSHIPING GOD is an experience that every believer needs to experience. My personal experience with GOD when I praise and worship HIM when I am alone with HIM cannot be measured. I feel the presence of GOD so mightily during my time with HIM. It is an experience that every child of GOD should experience. I am not the same when I worship and praise the LORD alone? Humble praise and worship please the LORD. HE delights in the love and devotion of HIS children. According to the Scriptures, the various expressions of praise bring blessings to the LORD. GOD eagerly awaits the fragrance of our affections, desiring to manifest HIS sweet presence and power in our midst. "The true worshipers shall worship the Father in spirit and in truth: for the Father seeketh such to worship him" (John 4:23).

PRAISE & WORSHIP BREAKS EVERY YOKE

From Old Testament to the New Testament, there has been occasions where Praising and Worshiping GOD has broken yokes and strong holds pulled down. For example, during the red sea crossing, Miriam and the women praise and worship the LORD. The women sand during the reign of King Jehoshaphat of Juda. Another New Testament story begins with the unjust arrest of Paul and Silas. Because they had cast a spirit of divination out of a girl, the local Philippian authorities beat them and then threw them into a jail cell. In addition to the trauma of the severe beating, they were fastened in stocks which clamped their arms and legs in an immovable position, causing cramps and loss of circulation. The situation was depressing. According to the standards of that day, a prison was more like the similarity of a dungeon. The place is dark, stench-ridden, damp, with no facility for toileting, or comforts of any kind. Yet, despite the excruciating pain in their bodies and the discouraging atmosphere, at midnight Paul and Silas were heard praying and singing praises to GOD! It was a strange sound to the other prisoners, who were used to only hearing the cries or cursing of those who had been beaten.

Then suddenly, there was an earthquake that shook the prison! The doors threw open, and remarkably, the bonds of Paul, Silas, and every other prisoner were released! What caused this mighty discharge of power? It is only the power Praising and Worshiping GOD. Acts 16:23-26 "And when they had laid many stripes on them, they threw them into prison, commanding the jailer to keep them securely. 24 Having received such a charge, he put them into the inner prison and fastened their feet in the stocks. 25 But at midnight Paul and Silas were praying and singing hymns to GOD, and the prisoners were listening to them.

{
Let everything that has breath praise the Lord
Praise the Lord!
(Psalm 150:6)
}

26 Suddenly there was a great earthquake, so that the foundations of the prison were shaken; and immediately all the doors were opened and everyone's chains were loosed."

PRAISE AND WORSHIP TAKES US INTO PRESENCE OF GOD!

Paul and Silas knew the secret of how to lift their hearts above their troubles and enter GOD'S presence and power. Through praise and worship their hearts were raised into the joyous presence and peace of GOD and provided GOD a channel for his power to operate in their circumstances. The Bible says that GOD inhabits in the praises of HIS people (Psalms 22:3). In other words, God "dwells" in the atmosphere of His praise. This means that praise is more than a reaction of coming into His presence. Praise to GOD is a vehicle of faith which takes us into HIS presence and power! PRAISE AND WORSHIP is the "gate-pass" which allows us to enter the holiness of HIS GLORY. The psalmist writes, "Enter into his gates with thanksgiving, and into his courts with praise: be thankful unto him and bless his name" (Psalms 100:4). When we are the presence of GOD, we are not thinking of anything about the world.

THE INFLUENCE OF PRAISE AND WORSHIP!

WHAT IS PRAISE? Praise means "to commend, to applaud or magnify." For the Christian, praise to God is an expression of worship, lifting-up and glorifying the Lord. It is an expression of humbling ourselves and centering our attention upon the Lord with heart-felt expressions of love, adoration, and thanksgiving. High praises bring our spirit into a pinnacle of fellowship and intimacy between ourselves and God — it magnifies our awareness of our spiritual union with the HIGHEST GOD. Praise transports us into the realm of the supernatural and into the power of God. "Blessed is the people that know the joyful sound: they shall walk, O LORD, in the light of thy countenance" (Psalms 89:15). Have you ever noticed when "gifts of the Spirit" operate in a church service? The power and anointing of the Holy Spirit usually become evident, after a time of worship and praise. Some think that worship is a response after the Holy Spirit moves upon them. However, it is the other way around. GOD'S presence responds when we move upon HIM with worship! Lifting JESUS CHRIST through praise and worship invokes the LORD'S presence and power to flow in our midst.

There are many actions involved with praise to GOD verbal expressions of adoration and thanksgiving, singing, playing instruments, shouting, dancing, lifting, or clapping our hands. But true praise is not "merely" going through these motions. Jesus spoke about the hypocrisy of the pharisees, whose worship was only an outward show and not from the heart. "This people draweth nigh unto me with their mouth, and honoureth me with their lips; but their heart is far from me" (Matthew 15:8). Genuine praise to GOD is a matter of humility and sincere devotion to the Lord from within. Unpretentious praise and worship please the LORD. HE delights in the love and devotion of HIS children. According to the scriptures, the various expressions of praise bring blessings to the LORD. HE eagerly awaits the fragrance of our affections, desiring to manifest His sweet presence and power in our midst. "the true worshipers shall worship the FATHER in spirit and in truth: for the FATHER seeketh such to worship him" (John 4:23).

> **But at midnight Paul and Silas were praying and singing hymns to God, and the prisoners were listening to them (Acts 16:25)**

PRAISE TO GOD IS A LIFESTYLE!

Praise is an expression of faith, and a declaration of victory! It declares that we believe God is with us and is in control of the outcome of all our circumstances (Romans 8:28). Praise is a "sacrifice," something that we offer to God sacrificially, not just because we feel like it, but because we believe in Him and wish to please Him. "By him therefore let us offer the sacrifice of praise to GOD continually, that is, the fruit of our lips giving thanks to his name" (Hebrews 13:15). All too often, praise to GOD is something that many people leave at church, an event that happens only when they come together with other Christians. However, praise should be a part of a believer's lifestyle, inter-mingled as a part of their daily prayer-life. At work, in the car, at home in bed, or anywhere; praise to the Lord brings the refreshment of the Lord's presence, along with HIS power and anointing. "I will bless the LORD at all times: his praise shall continually be in my mouth" (Psalms 34:1).

YOU PUT THE ENEMY RUNNING WHEN WE WORSHIP AND PRAISE GOD!

Since praise manifests GOD'S presence, we also realize that praise repels the presence of the enemy, Satan. An atmosphere which is filled with sincere worship and praise to GOD by humble and contrite hearts is disgusting to the Devil. He fears the power in the name of JESUS and flees from the LORD'S habitation in praise. "Whoso offereth praise glorifieth me: and to him that ordereth his conversation aright will I show the salvation of GOD" (Psalms 50:23). When the children of Judah found themselves outnumbered by the hostile armies of Ammon, Moab, and mount Seir, King Jehoshophat and all the people sought the Lord for His help. The LORD assured the people that this would be HIS battle. HE told them to go out against them, and HE would do the fighting for them. So, what did the children of Judah do?

Being the people of "praise" (Judah means Praise), and knowing that GOD manifests HIS power through praise, they sent their army against their enemies, led praises! So, on they went, ahead of the army declaring, "Praise the LORD, for HIS mercy endureth forever!" And the scripture says, "...when they began to sing and to praise, the LORD set ambushments against the children of Ammon, Moab, and mount Seir, which had come against Judah; and they were smitten" (2 Chronicles 20:22 NKJ). When GOD'S people begin to praise HIS name, it sends the enemy running! I challenge you to become a person of praise, and you will experience the release of the power of GOD! Please do not fail to praise and worship GOD in your time of distress. HE will come forth for you. I am a living testimony for what our GOD can do when we truly praise HIM in our hopeless and helpless situation. The truth is that Praising and worshiping GOD draws us closer to GOD. Praise and worshiping GOD is a vital way of getting close to GOD.

{ **Though the fig tree may not blossom, Nor fruit be on the vines; Though the labor of the olive may fail, And the fields yield no food; Though the flock may be cut off from the fold, And there be no herd in the stalls Yet I will rejoice in the Lord, I will joy in the God of my salvation (Habakkuk 3:17-18)** }

CHAPTER 22

THE CLOUD AND FIRE!

GOD Is A Covenant Keeping GOD!

GOD'S children today go through trials and temptations most of the time. To us, it seems that GOD does not care for us. This is a lie from the pit of hell. I am a living testimony of what GOD can do for us even in the presence of adversity. GOD is a loving father and a covenant keeping GOD. A promise keeper. The children of Israel were living in bondage in the land of Egypt for many years. They were afflicted physically and emotionally. They accepted their plight as their lot. Time came and GOD remembered them. GOD told Moses my name is "I AM WHO I AM." Over 350 years, GOD remembered the promises HE made to Abraham, Isaac, and Jacob. GOD saw the afflictions of HIS people. Unfortunately, Moses will have to face resistance from Pharoah, and he did. When God revealed HIMSELF to HIS people throughout the Old Testament, it was a divine manifestation of deity in sensible form. As we identified earlier, in the Old Testament, GOD manifested HIMSELF as a pillar of fire by night and cloud by day, shining light and providing protection for the people of GOD. In the New Testament, JESUS states HE IS THE "LIGHT OF THE WORLD." So, if GOD is a covenant keeping GOD, are we not to be faithful and obedient to HIM? We should obey HIM for who HE is.

Moses the greatest Prophets in the Old Testament was born of the Hebrew slaves and adopted by Pharoah's daughter. He chose to identify with his people. He did some thing that leaked to king Pharoah and as a result he left Egypt and he fled to Midian. One day he was tending the flock of Jethro his father in-law the priest of Midian. Moses took his flocks to Horeb, the mountain of GOD. Moses saw what he had never seen or heard before. The bush was burning with fire, but the bush was not consumed. He became curious to see what was going on. At this point, GOD revealed who HE was to Moses. "7 Then the Lord told him, "I have certainly seen the oppression of my people in Egypt. I have heard their cries of distress because of their harsh slave drivers. Yes, I am aware of their suffering. 8 So I have come down to rescue them from the power of the Egyptians and lead them out of Egypt into their own fertile and spacious land. It is a land flowing with milk and honey—the land where the Canaanites, Hittites, Amorites, Perizzites, Hivites, and Jebusites now live. 9 Look! The cry of the people of Israel has reached me, and I have seen how harshly the Egyptians abuse them. 10 Now go, for I am sending you to Pharoah. You must lead my people Israel out of Egypt" Exodus 3:7-10).

GOD'S purpose in sending the ten plagues upon Egypt was to convince Pharaoh to set the Hebrews free and allow them to worship GOD. What do I mean by Cloud and Fire? In the Old Testament, GOD used diverse ways to bring HIS children from Egypt to take them to the land HE promised their father Abraham, Isaac, and Jacob a land that HE will give them as an inheritance.

> And the Lord said: "I have surely seen the oppression of My people who are in Egypt, and have heard their cry because of their taskmasters, for I know their sorrows (Exodus 3:7).

To create that relationship, GOD had to first reveal HIMSELF. That was the purpose of the ten plagues – "So you will know that I am God" (Ex. 8:18). Each plague revealed some side of GOD'S mastery. For example, the plague of lice, which was the first plague that the Egypt sorcerers could not duplicate, showed that GOD had mastery over even the tiniest creations.

The relationship that GOD was establishing with the Israelites was a relationship of love. GOD has also established the same relationship with us when HE gave up HIS only begotten SON to be sacrificed on the Cross for us. Therefore, He had to show them that HE saw and cared about their afflictions. The Israelites had to feel taken care of by GOD. Relief from their suffering, freedom from their slavery, was not the goal of the Exodus, but was necessary for the purpose of establishing a relationship, is the true goal of the Exodus. GOD used ten different plaques as a sign that HE GOD wants Pharoh to let HIS people go because HE made covenant with Abraham their father. GOD used the List of the ten plagues of water turning blood, plague of frogs, plaque of lice, plaque of flies, plaques of livestock, plaque of boils, plaques of hail, plaques of locust, plaques of darkness and plaques of the death of firstborn.

Sadly, Pharaoh did not let the children of Israelites to go as GOD demanded and Egypt experienced extreme destruction because of the ten plagues (Exodus 7:14 to Exodus 12:36). One of the most interesting aspects of the Exodus from Egypt when the children of Israel came out from Pharaoh's oppression; there are other events that happened. GOD sent many plaques to tell Pharaoh that HE IS GOD of the Universe. GOD made Pharaoh that he will not stop HIM from fulfilling the promises HE made to Abraham, Isaac, and Jacob. God was tangibly with them as a cloud by day and a pillar of fire by night. I can only imagine how it would have felt to witness such glory and to perceptibly feel the presence of GOD with HIM, leading them where HE would. In the passage above, we see how the Israelites choose to move. When GOD moved, they move. When GOD stayed, they stayed. They followed the cloud and pillar of fire, never deviating from the path that GOD laid out for them. Without doubt, they had some knocks on the road as they have realized over the past weeks or so, but they still followed the cloud when GOD was present.

There is no question that GOD honors those who obey HIM and HIS WORD. GOD'S instructions need to be adhered to the core. At this point of the children of Israel journey, there was very anxious seeing the Egyptians soldiers coming after them. GOD used the Cloud by day to create a demarcation between them and their enemies. GOD used Fire by night to separate the children of Israel and the Egyptians army. GOD told Moses that HE has now seen the afflictions of HIS people in Egypt. HE promised Moses that HE would accomplish this because of the Oat HE made with Abraham, HIS friend. This is because Abraham was obedient to GOD in every way. GOD saw that Abraham can be trusted in carrying out instructions. The children were protected by clouds by day and pillars of fire by night. GOD is a way maker. HE is still making a way for us today.

 Who is like unto thee, O Lord, among the gods? who is like thee, glorious in holiness, fearful in praises, doing wonders? (Exodus 15:11) JESUS Is Our Pillar Of Cloud And Fire

Right after Adam and Eve sinned in the Garden of Eden, death came to the world. This was never GOD'S intention for humankind. For a long time, human beings were helpless and hopeless. At the right time, CHRIST came and died for the ungodly. For one will scarcely die for a righteous man: not even a good man that someone would venture even to die. Apostle Paul stated in the Book of Romans 5:6-10; "6 When we were utterly helpless, Christ came at just the right time and died for us sinners. 7 Now, most people would not be willing to die for an upright person, though someone might be willing to die for a person who is especially good. 8 But God showed his great love for us by sending Christ to die for us while we were still sinners. 9 And since we have been made right in God's sight by the blood of Christ, he will certainly save us from God's condemnation. 10 For since our friendship with God was restored by the death of his Son while we were still his enemies, we will certainly be saved through the life of his Son" (Romans 5:6-10 NLT).

Today, JESUS CHRIST is the pillar that holds our life from eternal destructions. HE IS OUR PILLAR OF CLOUD BY DAY AND PILLAR OF FIRE BY NIGHT. Since GOD is holy and just, CHRIST came to earth and accomplished HIS mission when HE physically died on the Cross and came back to life. Now, that it is an unbelievably loving action for GOD to do. Suppose a father went to the front of a car to rescue his daughter, we would say that the father is a brave father and that he loved his daughter. We might say that he loved his daughter so much and he was fearless in saving his daughter from death because of love. JESUS CHRIST did more than the earthly father. CHRIST left HIS throne in Heaven and came and died the death HE did not deserve. HE died on a cross to rescue us from hell or the Lake of Fire. Now that is love and kindness. HE is the GOOD SHEPARD, REDEEMER, SAVIOR OF THE WHOLE WORLD, FOUNTAIN OF LIFE, and OUR STONE OF HELP. All that is left is for you and me to believe HIM. Salvation by grace through faith in JESUS CHRIST is the main topic in the New Testament of the Bible. The Gospel is the good news of our reconciliation from the death of sin to eternal life in CHRIST. Learn more about the Biblical meaning of salvation with this collection of scripture quotes. May these Bible verses about salvation enlighten and inspire your faith and understanding of being saved.

In the New Testament, the LORD JESUS revealed HIMSELF as the "Light of the World", as the SAVIOR, and LORD of all those who received HIM through faith. New Testament passages such as Hebrews 12:1-2 reminds us to "fix our eyes on Jesus, the Author and Finisher of faith." The children of Israel fixed their eyes on the pillar of cloud at daytime, and the pillar of fire at nighttime.

Here we see JESUS manifesting HIMSELF as the "Pillar of Fire" by night; HE also appears as the "Pillar of Cloud" by day. GOD'S people wandering in the wilderness never had to worry about sunburn, exposure, and heat in the day. CHRIST is indeed the believer's SHEPHERD, LORD, KING, and DEFENDER THAT PROTECTS, and SHIELDS us, and averts any faith-destroying attacks from the enemy. Friends, let us move with the cloud. Do not be left behind but move with cloud. GOD is in the cloud. This is the cloud of deliverance, cloud of salvation, cloud of divine provision and cloud of protection from all the attack of Satan. You are about to be delivered from the bond and stronghold of the enemy of your soul.

 Who is like unto thee, O Lord, among the gods? who is like thee, glorious in holiness, fearful in praises, doing wonders? (Exodus 15:11)

CHAPTER 23

RUN TO THE END

Today, we have many skilled sports men and women. I have never been one of them. My alleged 'sports ability' is only playing long tennis with my husband in my leisure time only. I love to play tennis only when I have time to spare. I do not run, but I occasionally take a walk alone when I want to have fellowship with my HEAVENLY FATHER. I can appreciate Apostle Paul when he compares our Christian walk to a race, in the book of Hebrews, but it is not just ordinary race. It is a magnificent race to HEAVEN where multitudes that have gone on before are cheering us to run to the finish line of faith. Can you imagine that scene? Those who have gone before us are our cheer leaders, thriving on the sidelines encouraging me and you to make it to the end! The HOLY SPIRIT makes overcoming possible. Nothing is too difficult for us with the POWER of GOD working in our lives. Romans 8:26 tells us that GOD'S SPIRIT helps us in our weaknesses. Apostle Paul, who wrote the letter to the Romans, speaks for all of us when he said, "I can do all things through CHRIST who strengthens me" (Philippians 4:13). With JESUS in the vessel, we shall smile at the storm. We can run our Christian race to the end by the GRACE OF ALL AND MIGHTY GOD.

Rules to Run Our Christian Race of Faith

We are running not just escape hell fire. But we are running to spend eternity with CHRIST. HE did so much for us on the Cross of Calvary. HE paid the debt that he did not owe. And we owe the debt that we could not pay. The Scripture talks about laying aside every weight. What does it really mean to lay aside every weight? "Therefore, since we are surrounded by so great a cloud of witnesses, let us also lay aside every weight, and sin which clings so closely, and let us run with endurance the race that is set before us, looking to JESUS, the founder and perfecter of our faith, who for the joy that was set before HIM endured the cross, despising the shame, and is seated at the right hand of the throne of GOD.

Consider HIM who endured from sinners such hostility against HIMSELF, so that you may not grow weary or fainthearted" (Hebrews 12:1-3 ESV). For instance, when selecting clothing, sportspersons will make sure they are wearing weightless fabrics with the garments cut in a very efficient style. The clothing choice and cutting are vital, so the extra fabric does not grip the runner back. Also, there are things in our Christian walk that is not sin but that could weigh us down. The Greek word for weight is of any kind of a thing that is prominent extra bulk, extra mass, a burden, and something that burdens us. Is anything in our lives that is spiritually slowing you down? Are you clinging to something that you can cast along to the side of the road to quicken your speed? Do not delay. Tomorrow might be too late.

Casting off our sins! We must examine the motives of our hearts. This is especially important as the Scripture says that the heart is very wicked. Sin can be parceled in beautiful

But he who endures to the end shall be saved
(Matthew 24:13)

packaging. Everything might seem to be perfect from external appearances but what about the 'petite' sins? What about sinning in anger and smashing out at those we love? Do we discount it as a normal reaction? What about impatience? What about a root of bitterness that we have allowed to grow and flourish in our hearts towards family members, church family, or associates? Dear Brothers and Sisters, I challenge us all to cast it aside and reduce our load! (2 Timothy 2:15; Hebrews 10:36; 12:7). This was written to encourage and challenge all believers to persevere in their faith, especially during trials and persecution (2 Timothy 2:15; Hebrews 10:36; 12:7).

There is freedom and liberty in CHRIST. But it should not be abused. "I have fought the good fight, I have finished the race, I have kept the faith" (2Timothy 4:7, ESV). Run with endurance; you might feel like the last individual who was chosen to be on the crew but be assured that GOD chose YOU. Your speed might be slow, and you might be getting discouraged by other Christians who are racing ahead of you with speed and liveliness, but my brother or my sister, you are still in GOD'S Astonishing Race! GOD uses you right where you are so learning to be patient with yourself is necessary. In Greek, patience means steadfastness, constancy, and endurance. Beloved you are still in GOD'S Incredible Race! Do not give up!

Look unto JESUS; who are you looking to in your Faith? People will disappoint you, but JESUS will never let you down. Are you constantly looking at other runners and trying to catch up to them? Do you compare yourself with others? My siblings, are you? Let the LORD be your yardstick. "Don't you realize that in a race everyone runs, but only one person gets the prize? So run to win!" (1 Corinthians 9:24NLT). I am sure you have heard of an innovator. An innovator is one who runs next to you, sets your pace, so you do not exhaust yourself before you have time to far-reach your race. There are those that start big and end up being put aside because they use up all their energy before the finish line. Sad to say, it is typically the ones that we are trying to keep up with or equate ourselves with. JESUS is our pacesetter. Do not get ahead of HIM and keep your eyes on HIM!

WHAT DOES IT REAL MEAN TO "RUN THE RACE SET BEFORE US" (HEBREWS 12:1)?

Run the race set before us! What kind of race does CHRIST followers run? Who sets the race parameters? Is it a race we define and a purpose for ourselves? Athletes in a race were surrounded by rows and rows of spectators pictured for us as "a great cloud of witnesses." "Since we are surrounded by such a great cloud of witnesses, let us throw off everything that hinders and the sin that so easily entangles. And let us run with perseverance the race marked out for us"

WHAT DOES IT REAL MEAN TO "RUN THE RACE SET BEFORE US" (HEBREWS 12:1)?

(Hebrews 12:1). The "witnesses" of the believers' race are listed in the previous chapter of Hebrews: the people of GOD whose faithful lives were recorded in the Old Testament.

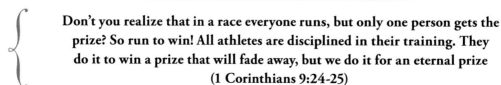

> Don't you realize that in a race everyone runs, but only one person gets the prize? So run to win! All athletes are disciplined in their training. They do it to win a prize that will fade away, but we do it for an eternal prize (1 Corinthians 9:24-25)

These saints persevered despite inconceivable oppression and brutality (Hebrews 11:33–38) and were commended for their faithfulness. Whether the saints of Hebrews 11 are watching us run our "race" today is unsure; the point of the passage is that their testimony lives on. Their unbending faith bears witness to the assurances of JESUS CHRIST, urging us to follow their pattern and "run with perseverance the race marked out for us" (Hebrews 12:1). The "race," then, is the Believers life. It is a marathon, not a dash and we are called to stay on the course and remain faithful to the end. Apostle Paul used these same images near the end of his life: "I have fought the good fight, I have finished the race, and I have kept the faith" (2 Timothy 4:7).

The commitment of the Old Testament "witnesses" speaks to CHRIST followers today of the rewards of remaining in the race, of never giving up (1 Corinthians 9:24; Philippians 3:14). A marathon is an energetic test of fitness and stamina. The race set before us have need of faith, endurance, commitment, and persuasion to live faithfully (1 Corinthians 9:25–26; Philippians 3:12–14; 1 Timothy 6:12). The race is "set before us;" we did not select the course, for it is GOD who established it. This race we run for CHRIST. We stay the course in vindictiveness of trials and persecutions (Hebrews 12:4–11). As we run, we must "fix our eyes on JESUS, the author and perfecter of our faith" (Hebrews 12:2). Because He perfectly finished HIS race, CHRIST IS THE FOCUS OF OUR LIVES. We look away from all distractions because HE is already at the finish line (Lamentations 3:25; Matthew 6:33; Romans 2:7).

The race demands that we do away with "everything that hinders" sin and whatever else threatens our relationship with GOD (Hebrews 12:1). Anything that will slow us down or trip up us must be cast off. The apostle Paul says, "to put off your old self, which is being corrupted by its deceitful desires; to be made new in the attitude of your minds; and to put on the new self, created to be like God in true righteousness and holiness" (Ephesians 4:22–24). With the encouragement of those who have gone on before, we rid ourselves of thoughts, attitudes, and habits that impede our progress (Romans 12:2; Titus 3:3; 1 Peter 1:14). Seeing that the race GOD set out for us is a lifelong marathon, we must commit ourselves to run to the very end. A daily regimen of prayer, worship, reading GOD'S WORD and examining our lives for impediments will help. We will persevere by maintaining a CHRIST like attitude even during trials (1 Peter 2:21; 4:1; 1 John 2:6). No matter how long the race may be, we keep our eyes on JESUS, "the champion who initiates and perfects our faith" (Hebrews 12:2, NLT). There is joy waiting for each one of us who perseveres to the end.

FINISH YOUR CHRISTIAN RACE WELL!

Siblings, finishing our Christian race well can never involve looking back. Looking back implies our heart and our desires and our loves are all still back at the starting line, and not in the kingdom of GOD. When we look back, we reveal that we belong with the world and the things of the world, and not with the world to come. And if we belong to the world, what will eventually become of us? (Suggestion: read the story about Lot's wife it is a scary thing to look back!). This implies we have already begun our race, and now that we have, we must continually keep our stare fixed forward or upward as opposed to backward. We are not to look back on the things that we have left behind, or the weight of sin that we have cast off. They are in the dirt and dust where they belong, whereas we are headed for glory. The Book Colossians offers similar advice for the Christian life: "If then you have been raised with CHRIST, seek the things that are above, where CHRIST is, seated at the right hand of GOD. Set your minds on things that are above, not on things that are on earth. For we have died, and our life is hidden with CHRIST in GOD (Colossians 3:1–3).

{ **Don't you realize that in a race everyone runs, but only one person gets the prize? So run to win! All athletes are disciplined in their training. They do it to win a prize that will fade away, but we do it for an eternal prize (1 Corinthians 9:24-25)** }

The point that Apostle Paul is making here is quite plain: our destination is in the heavenly places, where even now we are spiritually raised with CHRIST. And if that is our ultimate destination, we need to keep our focus on the things that are above. We belong above in HEAVEN, not below on earth. JESUS HIMSELF says the same thing in Luke 9: "No one who puts his hand to the plow and looks back is fit for the KINGDOM OF GOD" (v. 62). Let us run toward HEAVEN by keeping the eyes of our heart fixed on the one who is already there; the one who has already run the race and come in first. JESUS CHRIST stands victorious in the heavenly places and is waiting to share that victory with us when we see HIM face to face. Let us keep our minds and hearts fixated on Christ, who holds the prize at the finish line—and he is the prize.

In conclusion, we want to consider the most important aspect of running our Christian race well: keeping our eyes on the prize. Yes, we need proper motivation and encouragement to run, we need to free ourselves of things that would hinder our progress, and we need to prepare for the long haul. But none of these matters if we do not keep our eyes on the prize. In this case, which does not mean a medal or a finish line? It means "looking to JESUS." When Paul says, "I have finished the race" (2 Timothy 4:7), obviously he was talking about motion. And perseverance means to keep going despite obstacles. So, when Paul says, "I have finished the race," he was saying, "I have persevered." We do need to stand firm, and Scripture repeatedly exhorts us to stand firm. But remember, that is more than just standing still. If we get that idea, we have missed the point. We must move forward. We must persevere. We must be like Paul and say, "I have fought the good fight, I have finished the race, I have kept the faith." May you and I be like the Apostle Paul.

Notice that Apostle Paul is confident that he belongs to CHRIST ("CHRIST JESUS made me HIS own"), but he does not set his sight on past experiences ("forgetting what lies behind"); rather he aims at his future with CHRIST, even "straining forward to what lies ahead." The author of Hebrews exhorts us to press ahead in our Christian life when he writes, "For we have come to share in CHRIST, if indeed we hold our original confidence firm to the end" (Heb 3:15). JESUS urged HIS disciples not to neglect their perseverance when people around them were giving up on CHRIST or turning to counterfeits: And then many will fall away and betray one another and hate one another. And many false prophets will arise and lead many astray. And because lawlessness will increase, the love of many will grow cold. But the one who endures to the end will be saved (Matthew 24:10-12).

It is enticing, once we've reputable good beginning, to ease back a little and fail to finish what we have started. As we have observed this in day-to-day practical experience, this can happen in one-on-one football or soccer tournaments between friends/associates. Nonetheless most significantly, it can happen in our Christian lives. But then again GOD has given us everything we need to finish our race well. The Scripture is there for us, the Body of CHRIST, for instances, those who went previously ahead of us and remained faithful up until the end. Let us grab a hold of these resources and recover our pace so that we can someday say with Paul, "I have fought the good fight, I have finished the race, I have kept the faith" (2 Tim 4:7). For example, Apostle Paul and Demas were associates in the ministry of CHRIST; then there's Demas, Paul's ministry companion who eventually left CHRIST for the pleasures of this world (2 Tim 4:10). Speaking, what gives the impression of a strong start does not continuously interpret into a strong finish.

 Don't you realize that in a race everyone runs, but only one person gets the prize? So run to win! All athletes are disciplined in their training. They do it to win a prize that will fade away, but we do it for an eternal prize (1 Corinthians 9:24-25)

CHAPTER 24

CONCLUSION

In summary of the question of, "How Many Believers Will Make Heaven" is a vital question. This question is really complicated for me to answer. I am the least person for this kind of question to come to. No human being in this world can answer this question. I have no idea who will make HEAVEN or who will not make HEAVEN! Is only JESUS CHRIST WHO IS QUALIFIED TO CORRECTLY ANSWER THIS QUESTION! But I am encouraging and calling all believers in CHRIST to keep making progress in our faith and not to allow spiritual stagnation to settle into our lives. Even though our genuine faith in CHRIST is protected and cannot be lost (John 10:27-30; Rom 8:28-39), the same GOD who provides us with a secure salvation also provides us the means to keep believing. What are the Biblical strategies we can implement to make sure we finish well? Hold onto Believing the WORD OF GOD and Repenting of Your Sins.

Brothers and sisters, the spirit of rejecting our Biblical principles is unbelief. The cure to publicly rejection of Christian doctrines, therefore, is faith. Israel fell away from GOD and came under HIS judgment because they failed to receive GOD'S WORD by faith (Heb 4:2). The author of Hebrews, as he feared his listeners were in danger of falling away from CHRIST, repeatedly exhorted them to keep believing in GOD'S promises and repenting from the sin that saddled them with spiritual difficulty (Hebrew 10:19-25). In our reading of Scripture and listening to preaching and teaching, we need to fire ourselves up against apostasy when we carefully engross the truth we hear and use that truth to exacerbate specific repentance in our lives.

The good news is GOD wants to help us. The truth is that GOD sent HIS SON JESUS to fix our problem. The Bible says, "This is how much GOD loved the world: HE gave HIS SON, HIS ONE and only SON. And this is why: so that no one will spend eternity in hell; by believing in HIM, anyone can have a whole and eternal life. GOD sent HIS SON because HE loves us that was why HE sent HIS SON to reconcile to HIMSELF and not merely to point an accusing finger, telling the world how bad it was. HE came to help, to put the world right again." (John 3:16-17). JESUS came to resolve our problem and provide us the fullest life possible. The fact is that JESUS came and offered everyone a fresh start, a new life. We Christians call this being "born again," or "salvation." Being born again involves acknowledging that your present way of living is not working. Instead of doing what you have always done, JESUS invites us to experience a new way of living - HIS way. It is about making JESUS the leader of our life and inviting HIS HOLY SPIRIT to begin changing us from inside out; to make us more like JESUS. Being born again is not something you earn; it is a gift from GOD. HE hopes every person on earth will accept HIS invitation to this new life.

Not everyone who says to Me, 'Lord, Lord,' shall enter the kingdom of heaven, but he who does the will of My Father in heaven (Matthew 7:21)

89

According to the WORD OF JESUS CHRIST HIMSELF, "MANY ARE CALLED, BUT FEW ARE CHOSEN." (Matthew 22:14). It is only the SWORD OF THE SPIRIT that will enlighten us on the standard of who qualifies to go to Heaven? It is not late my dear friends; you can amend your ways to be a candidate for this glorious place called HEAVEN where we will be with JESUS CHRIST OUR LORD forever and ever. If you have given your life to CHRIST in the past and backslide, ask GOD to forgive you and plead with the HOLY SPIRIT to give you strength to start afresh to make things right with GOD.

This question of How Many Believers Will Make HEAVEN is a very thought-provoking question. Our existence's objective and our first main concern should be to know GOD. How much do we know GOD and obey HIM for us to be accepted or qualified to make HEAVEN? Believers today are facing a lot of challenges. Our faith in CHRIST has been challenged not only from individual citizens, but from those in authority (elected officials). Evil legislations have been put together just to weaken the Body of CHRIST. Evil has now been accepted and embraced as good and righteousness is now regarded as evil. There are evil rising tides against the Church of JESUS CHRIST. The Church needs to wake up from sleep and fight. "And from the days of John the Baptist until now the Kingdom of Heaven suffers violence and the violent take it by force.

The definitive goal of every Believer is to get to know GOD. These beliefs are substantiated in many verses in the Scripture. "This is eternal life that they may know you the only true God and Jesus Christ whom You have sent" (John 17:3). "Let him who glories glory in this – that he understands and knows Me" (Jer. 9:24). "That I may know Him" (Phil 3:10). Other key verses include Daniel 11:32, John 14:7, Phil 3:8, Col 1:10, 2 Peter3:18 and 1 John 5:20.

It is attention-grabbing that the HOLY SPIRIT uses the word "know" many times in the Scripture to explain the relationship, and responsibility, which GOD requires of us. The Bible teaches us that GOD wants us to KNOW HIM. "Know" is a word used so frequently in social relationships. The definition from the dictionary put it, in this setting, as "to be familiar with," or "to be on close terms with." It is possible for us to get to know people, to become conversant with them and to become friendly with them. In what way do we do this? By what means do we get to know people we have not known? By what method do we get to know people we already know better? For example, we understand this process on a social level, the HOLY SPIRIT helps us to comprehend what we must do to get to know GOD on a spiritual level, and by what means to get to know HIM better. We must, however, always remember that getting to know GOD better is, as in human relationships, a slow, and even a lifetime, procedure which involves time, patience as well as honesty.

Envisage that you want to know and become familiar and sociable with a certain individual you have never met; or envision that you want to increase your knowledge of, and intimacy with, or somebody you already know. The question then is what steps would you like to take? You should be knowledgeable about his or her character, his or her entire make up. You could find, read, and study any information which is written about your impending friend. So, for us to know GOD, we need to study what the Bible says about HIM. Our knowledge of GOD will be based on the truths we learn about HIM. As you take time to be with GOD, study the WORD OF GOD, which is the SWORD OF THE SPIRIT, Do not just read the WORD of GOD but study it, meditate on HIS WORD daily, and be still in HIS presence, your knowledge of HIM will grow and HIS JOY will be your strength.

 Not everyone who says to Me, 'Lord, Lord,' shall enter the kingdom of heaven, but he who does the will of My Father in heaven (Matthew 7:21)

The purpose of this Book is to bring to our attention that not all that claim to be Christians will go to HEAVEN, "Not everyone who calls out to me, 'Lord! Lord!' will enter the Kingdom of Heaven. Only those who do the will of my Father in heaven will enter. 22 On judgment day many will say to me, Lord! Lord! We prophesied in your name and cast out demons in your name and performed many miracles in your name.' 23 But I will reply, I never knew you. Get away from me, you who break God's laws" (Matthew 7:21-23). It is encouraging believers to get close to GOD if we want to make HEAVEN. CHRIST is the LIGHT of the world.

JESUS is the LIGHT; we HIS followers are required to live in the LIGHT which is CHRIST the LORD. There is no debate concerning this! According to the Book of Ephesians 5:1-12; "Follow God's example in everythng you do, because you are His dear children. 2 Live a life filled with love for others, following the example of Christ who loved you and gave himself as a sacrifice to take away your sins. And God was please because that sacrifice was like sweet perfume to him. 3 Let there be no sexual immorality impurity, or greed among you. Such sins have no place among God's people. 4 Obscene stories, foolish talk, and coarse jokes—these are not for you. Instead, let there be thankfulness to God. 5 You can be sure that no immoral, impure, or greedy person will inherit the Kingdom of Christ and of God. For a greedy person is really an idolater who worships the things of this world. 6 Do not be fooled by those who try to excuse these sins, for the terrible anger of God comes upon all those who disobey him. 7 Do not participate in the things these people do. 8 For though your hearts were once full of darkness, now you are full or light from the Lord, and your behavior should show it! 9 For this light

within you produces only what is good, right, and true. 10 Try to find out what is pleasing to the Lord. 11 Thake no part in the worthless deeds of evil and darkness; instead, rebuke and expose them. 12 It is shameful even to talk about the things that ungodly people do in secret" (Ephesians 5:1-12).

What Do We Do To Go To HEAVEN?

We need to believe and allow the HOLY SPIRIT to direct us in all areas of our life. Besides the HOLY SPIRIT intervening on our behalf and guiding us, the HOLY SPIRIT can also lead us if we allow HIM. The HOLY SPIRIT is the third member of the TRINITY, which means HE is GOD. Many people do not know that the HOLY SPIRIT is GOD, but HE is GOD. There are times in our lives when we feel overcome with sadness, discomfort, and sorrow. Most of the time, we may not know how to express our emotional state much less express them in words. In believers' lives, this is time we need the HOLY SPIRIT more.

It is the HOLY SPIRIT who can intervene on our behalf. HOLY SPIRIT will communicate state of mind to the FATHER. Have faith in GOD. From the time a person places faith in Christ, they are given the Holy Spirit. The Holy Spirit permanently indwells believers, and He will never leave us. Jesus referred to the Holy Spirit as "the Helper" (John 14:26, ESV). He is referred to as "the Helper" because He helps us in our struggles. "When we don't know what to pray for, the Holy Spirit intercedes with moans and groans that words cannot express" (Romans 8:26).

Not everyone who says to Me, 'Lord, Lord,' shall enter the kingdom of heaven, but he who does the will of My Father in heaven (Matthew 7:21)

To go to HEAVEN, we need to stay away from living in the flesh. The Sinful Flesh: Due to our fallen nature, we all have sinful flesh (Romans 3:23). This means we are all born into sin and we all effortlessly sin. The sinful nature stays with us until we die. Many Christians believe a person's sinful flesh is destroyed once they place faith in Christ; however, this is not true. When a person places faith in Christ, they are forgiven of their sins, yet their sin nature is not completely eradicated. Our sinful nature will not be eradicated until we are with Christ in heaven. Since we will continue to struggle with our sinful flesh throughout our earthly lives, we are constantly being tempted by our sinful nature. Our sinful flesh wants us to follow it rather than to follow the HOLY SPIRIT.

When we choose to follow the HOLY SPIRIT, then we are not walking in accordance with the flesh. (Galatians 5:16-2). Following the lead of the HOLY SPIRIT can be hard, but it is completely worth it. It is important to note that if we are not being led by the HOLY SPIRIT, then we are being led by our own sinful nature. As Christians, we must take the active decision to choose to follow the lead of the Holy Spirit rather than our sinful flesh. When we stand before GOD one day, we might not be able ask for entry to HEAVEN based on our personal merit. We have nothing to offer. Compared to GOD'S standard of holiness, none of us is good enough. But JESUS is, and it is by CHRIST merit we can enter HEAVEN. First Corinthians 6:9-11 say, "Do you not know that wrongdoers will not inherit the kingdom of God? Do not be deceived: Neither the sexually immoral nor idolaters nor adulterers nor men who have sex with men nor thieves nor the greedy nor drunkards nor slanderers nor swindlers will inherit the kingdom of God. And that is what some of us were. "Do not copy the behaviors and customs of this world, but let God transform you into a new person by changing the way you think. Then you will learn to know God's will for you, which is good, pleasing, and perfect" (Romans 12:2). But be transformed by the renewing of your mind means GOD'S transformation within the mind of a believer through the help of the HOLY SPIRIT. This is a command from GOD. If we want to be like HIM, we must be ready to be transformed and we will be blessed for it.

Who Will Go To Heaven?

The people who go to heaven are alike in one way: they are sinners who have placed their faith in the Lord Jesus Christ (John 1:12; Acts 16:31; Romans 10:9). They have recognized their need for a Savior and humbly accepted God's offer of forgiveness. They have repented of their old ways of living and set their course to follow Christ (Mark 8:34; John 15:14). They have not attempted to earn God's forgiveness but have served him gladly from grateful hearts (Psalm 100:2). The kind of faith that saves a soul is one that transforms a life (James 2:26; 1 John 3:9-10) and rests fully on the grace of God. There is one portion in the Bible that makes me wonder of all about who makes HEAVEN or not? "Enter by the narrow gate; for wide is the gate and broad is the way that leads to destruction, and there are many who go in by it. Because narrow is the gate and difficult is the way which leads to life, and there are few who find it." (Matthew 7:13-14). This verse is even more thoughtful when observed over the lens of this one. JESUS is.

Today, some Believers are meandering with the gospel. My observation with some Believers shows the truth about how Christianity in this age group is being move away by those who want to believe that they can agree to take the message of tolerance and inclusion and still be faithful CHRIST followers. It is impossible. Let us look at what CHRIST HIMSELVE said in Mark 7:20-23; "And then he added, "It is what comes from inside that defiles you. 21 For from within, out of a person's heart, come evil thoughts, sexual immorality, theft, murder, twenty-two adultery, greed, wickedness, deceit, lustful desires, envy, slander, pride, and foolishness. 23 All these vile things come from within; they are what defile you." (Mark 7:20-23).

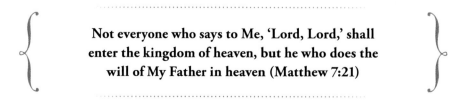

> **Not everyone who says to Me, 'Lord, Lord,' shall enter the kingdom of heaven, but he who does the will of My Father in heaven (Matthew 7:21)**

The fact is that we can be sure that all who practice these things will not enter HEAVEN. Some Believers can accept abortion and same-sex marriage and still claim to be Christian. This is a lie from the pit of hell. But the good news is that there is still time to repent. Our HEAVENLY FATHER is a merciful GOD, HE will forgive you and make you whole. They attended church. They claimed to be Christians. But Jesus' words here are chilling, "I tell you I don't know you, where you are from." It is not enough to self-identify as a Christian. In fact, it is not even enough to attend church for years, fellowshipping with other Christians; and doing all kinds of Christian things. Entrance into heaven is not based on a prayer, church attendance, and doing "Christian things."

Entrance into heaven is based on this one thing alone: A personal relationship with JESUS CHRIST that grows out of our acceptance of HIS sacrifice for our sins and our submission to the precepts and principles of HIS WORD. Salvation does not happen with just prayer. Salvation happens when we put our faith in JESUS CHRIST and HIS shed BLOOD for our sin. This act of faith initiates the change that begins in the heart of a new believer in CHRIST. "Believe on the Lord Jesus Christ, and you will be saved, you and your household." (Acts16:31). The truth is that not all Christians are true believers.

Dear friends, my prayer here is that each one of us who professed JESUS CHRIST as his or her LORD and SAVIOUR will run this race to the end. There are so many distractions throughout the world today; but do not allow yourself to be deceived. There are many fake preachers today. CHRIST is coming back to judge the world. The question of how many believers will make it to HEAVEN is an important question. In the book of the gospel of Matthew 24:13 NKV; It says, "But he who endures to the end shall be saved." THE WORD OF GOD encourages us to run to receive a prize. "Don't you realize that in a race everyone runs, but only one person gets the prize? So run to win! All athletes are disciplined in their training. They do it to win a prize that will fade away, but we do it for an eternal prize (1 Corinthians 9:24-25). The bottom line here is that we should all endeavor to attend the invitation of the LAMB SUPPER. The LAMB MARRIAGE SUPPER is going to be glorious and unimaginable experience seeing JESUS face to face. It is going to be a life event that none of us would want to miss it.

The MARRIAGE SUPPER of the LAMB is a representative picture of the overjoyed, close, and everlasting fellowship that takes place between JESUS CHRIST (the LAMB OF GOD) and HIS bride (the BODY OF CHRIST). John, the beloved among all the disciples, saw a lot when he was on the Island of Patmos. "Then I heard the voice of a great multitude, like the roar of many waters and like the sound of mighty peals of thunder, crying out, "Hallelujah! For the Lord, our God the Almighty reigns. Let us rejoice and exult and give HIM all the glory, for the marriage of the Lamb has come, and his Bride has made herself ready; It had granted her to clothe herself with fine linen, bright and pure for the fine linen is the righteous deeds of the saints. And the angel said to me, Write this: Blessed are those who are invited to the marriage supper of the Lamb. And he said to me, These are the true words of God" (Revelation 19:6-9 ESV). Work hard so you will attend this HOLY WEDDING INVITATION. Imagine we will all be hugged by the LORD JESUS HIMSELF. Run to win a crown. Do not stop this race halfway; until we hear well done my faithful servant takes a place prepared for you.

Not everyone who says to Me, 'Lord, Lord,' shall enter the kingdom of heaven, but he who does the will of My Father in heaven (Matthew 7:21)

Dear brothers, sisters, and friends' life is meaningless without CHRIST JESUS. On the other hand, life is meaningful with GOD THE FATHER, GOD THE SON, AND GOD THE HOLY SPIRIT. All true believers have hope in the resurrection and our life with GOD in the new Heavens and the new earth. As I am authoring this book, my heart is broken because of what is going on in the whole world. To GOD ALONE BE ALL THE GLORY because we are not hopeless because JESUS CHRIST have gone to prepare a place for all believers where we are going to spend eternity with HIM forever.

{ **Not everyone who says to Me, 'Lord, Lord,' shall enter the kingdom of heaven, but he who does the will of My Father in heaven (Matthew 7:21)** }

ABOUT THE AUTHOR

Dorothy came from a polygamous family. She loves the LORD. Accept CHRIST AS HER LORD in November of 1974. She is very enthusiastic about missions. She has been to Burundi in Central Africa, Ecuador in South America, and Nigeria in West Africa multiple times on mission trip.

Dorothy worked as a medical director for African Christian Fellowship Midwest Region for four years. She worked as children and youth director for 6 years. She also served in African Christian Fellowship USA as the youth and young adult over 10 years as the councilor. Was the Secretary for two terms in African Christian Fellowship Chicago North?

She has been a professional Registered Nurse for over 30 years. She is Executive Director and Founder of New Hope HIV/AIDS Education/ Prevention (A USA based non-profit organization). She is a business consultant, a motivational speaker, an encourager, and a prayer warrior. Mrs. Princewill is still a committed member of African Christian Fellowship USA. She is currently the Program Coordinator for Women of Divine Purpose; a women's prayer group based in Chicago, Illinois. She is a member of Wailing Women Worldwide.

Mrs. Princewill has been married to the husband of her youth for 45 years. She has three grown sons. Two GOD given daughters. Have many grandchildren and thirteen GOD Children. A member of Assembly of GOD Church since her conversion and have served in different capacities of the Church.

Printed in the United States
by Baker & Taylor Publisher Services